Real-time Analytics with Storm and Cassandra

Solve real-time analytics problems effectively using Storm and Cassandra

Shilpi Saxena

BIRMINGHAM - MUMBAI

Real-time Analytics with Storm and Cassandra

First published: March 2015

Production reference: 1240315

Published by Packt Publishing Ltd.
Livery Place
35 Livery Street
Birmingham B3 2PB, UK.

ISBN 978-1-78439-549-0

www.packtpub.com

Credits

Author

Shilpi Saxena

Reviewers

Sourav Gulati

Saurabh Gupta

Ranjeet Kumar Jha

Mark Kerzner

Sonal Raj

Commissioning Editor

Akram Hussain

Acquisition Editor

Larissa Pinto

Content Development Editor

Shweta Pant

Technical Editor

Saurabh Malhotra

Copy Editors

Pranjali Chury

Merilyn Pereira

Project Coordinator

Shipra Chawhan

Proofreaders

Simran Bhogal

Maria Gould

Paul Hindle

Indexer

Mariammal Chettiyar

Graphics

Sheetal Aute

Valentina D'silva

Abhinash Sahu

Production Coordinator

Manu Joseph

Cover Work

Manu Joseph

About the Author

Shilpi Saxena is a seasoned professional, who is leading in management with an edge of being a technology evangelist. She is an engineer who has exposure to a variety of domains (machine to machine space, health care, telecom, hiring, and manufacturing). She has experience in all aspects of conception and execution of enterprise solutions. She has been architecting, managing and delivering solutions in the big data space for the last 3 years, handling high performance geographically distributed teams of elite engineers.

Shilpi has more than 12 years (3 years in the big data space) of experience in development and execution of various facets of enterprise solutions both in product/services dimensions of the software industry. An engineer by degree and profession, she has worn varied hats — developer, technical leader, product owner, tech manager, and so on, and she has seen all flavors the industry has to offer.

She has architected and worked through some of the pioneers' production implementation in big data on Storm and Impala with auto scaling in AWS.

To know more about her, visit her LinkedIn profile at `http://in.linkedin.com/pub/shilpi-saxena/4/552/a30`.

I would like to thank my husband, Sachin Saxena, and my mother, Manju Saxena, for their constant support and encouragement while writing this book. A sincere word of thanks to Impetus and all my mentors, who gave me a chance to innovate and learn as part of the big data group.

About the Reviewers

Sourav Gulati is an MCA and has been working in the IT industry for about 5 years. He has worked on technologies such as Java and Unix shell scripting and has also worked on big data technologies such as Hadoop, Cassandra, Storm, and so on. Initially, he started working for Tech Mahindra in 2010 and then moved to Impetus in 2012. Currently, he is working as a senior software engineer at Impetus.

> I would really like to thank Shilpi Saxena and Packt Publishing for giving me the chance to be a part of this book. This book is packed with practical knowledge and experience. I would also like to wish Shilpi a lot of success with this book.

Saurabh Gupta is the lead software engineer at Impetus Technologies and has around 8 years of experience in IT. He started his career with Java/J2EE and headed toward NoSQL and big data technologies. He loves to read about new technologies or tools on the market. He believes that there are no secrets to success, but rather that it is the result of preparation, hard work, and learning from failure.

> I want to thank my wife, Nalini, and the rest of my family, who supported and encouraged me in spite of all the time it kept me away from them.

Ranjeet Kumar Jha has over 12 years of experience in various phases of project life cycles, including the development and design phases, and has also been part of production support for Java/J2EE and big data-based applications. He has more than 6 years of experience as a technical architect in Java technologies and more than 3 years in big data stacks. He has worked in various domains such as finance, insurance, e-commerce, digital media, and online advertisements.

Ranjeet has worked as a programmer, designer, and mentor and now works as an architect in all types of projects related to Java, especially J2EE and big data.

His LinkedIn profile is available at https://www.linkedin.com/in/jharanjeet.

His certifications include:

- OCM-JEA 5 (Oracle Certified Master, Java Enterprise Architect) with a 94 percent score in 2011
- OCE-WSD (Oracle Certified Expert, JAVA EE 6 Web Services Developer) in 2013
- SCJP (Sun Certified Java Programmer) in 2004
- SCWCD (Sun Certified Web Component Developer) in 2004
- Java Development with Apache Cassandra from DataStax in 2014
- MongoDB for Java Developers from MongoDB University in 2014

The companies he has worked for include the following:

- EtechAces Consulting and Marketing Pvt Ltd. Gurgaon (Delhi NCR)
- Times Internet Ltd (TimesGroup), Noida (Delhi NCR)
- Ebusinessware Inc (now Xoriant Corporation), Gurgaon (Delhi NCR)
- WIPRO, Gurgaon (Delhi NCR)
- AgreeYa Solution Pvt Ltd, Noida (Delhi NCR)
- INCA Informatics, Noida (Delhi NCR)

I would like to thank my family — my wife, Anila Jha, and two kids, Anushka Jha and Tanisha Jha, for their constant support, encouragement, and patience. Without you, I wouldn't have achieved so much! Love you all immensely.

Mark Kerzner holds degrees in law, math, and computer science. He is a software architect who has been working on Hadoop-based systems since 2008. Mark is a cofounder of Elephant Scale, a big data training and consulting company. He is a coauthor of the open source books *Hadoop Illuminated* and *Hbase Design Patterns*, both by Packt Publishing. He has also authored and coauthored other books and patents, which can be found at http://www.amazon.com.

I would like to acknowledge the help of my colleagues, in particular, Sujee Maniyam, and last but not least, my multitalented family.

Sonal Raj is a hacker, Pythonista, big data believer, and a technology dreamer. He has a passion for design and is an artist at heart. He blogs about technology, design, and gadgets at http://www.sonalraj.com/. When not working on projects, he can be found traveling, stargazing, or reading.

He has pursued engineering in computer science and loves to work on community projects. He has been a research fellow at SERC, IISc, Bangalore, and has taken up projects on graph computations using Neo4j and Storm. Sonal has been a speaker at PyCon India and local meets on Neo4j and has also published articles and research papers in leading magazines and international journals. He has contributed to several open source projects.

Sonal has been actively involved in the development of machine learning frameworks and has worked on technologies such as NoSQL databases including MongoDB and streaming using Apache Spark. He is currently working at Goldman Sachs.

I am grateful to the author for patiently listening to my critiques and I'd like to thank the open source community for keeping their passion alive and contributing to such remarkable projects. A special thank you to my parents, without whom I would never have grown to love learning as much as I do.

www.PacktPub.com

Support files, eBooks, discount offers, and more

For support files and downloads related to your book, please visit www.PacktPub.com.

Did you know that Packt offers eBook versions of every book published, with PDF and ePub files available? You can upgrade to the eBook version at www.PacktPub.com and as a print book customer, you are entitled to a discount on the eBook copy. Get in touch with us at service@packtpub.com for more details.

At www.PacktPub.com, you can also read a collection of free technical articles, sign up for a range of free newsletters and receive exclusive discounts and offers on Packt books and eBooks.

https://www2.packtpub.com/books/subscription/packtlib

Do you need instant solutions to your IT questions? PacktLib is Packt's online digital book library. Here, you can search, access, and read Packt's entire library of books.

Why subscribe?

- Fully searchable across every book published by Packt
- Copy and paste, print, and bookmark content
- On demand and accessible via a web browser

Free access for Packt account holders

If you have an account with Packt at www.PacktPub.com, you can use this to access PacktLib today and view 9 entirely free books. Simply use your login credentials for immediate access.

Table of Contents

Preface

Storm, initially a project from the house of Twitter, has graduated to the league of Apache and thus rechristened from Twitter Storm. It is the brainchild of Nathan Marz that's now adopted by leagues of Cloudera's Distribution Including Apache Hadoop (CDH) and the Hortonworks Data Platform (HDP), and so on.

Apache Storm is a highly scalable, distributed, fast, and reliable real-time computing system designed to process very high velocity data. Cassandra complements the computing capability by providing lightning-fast read and writes, and this is the best combination currently available for data storage with Storm.

The combination of the Storm computing and Cassandra storage is helping technology evangelists to solve various business problems involving complex and high data volume situations such as real-time customer service, dashboards, security, sensor data analysis, data monetization, and so on.

This book will equip users with the capability to harness the processing power of Storm in combination with the speed and reliability of Cassandra to develop production-grade enterprise solutions on real-time use cases.

What this book covers

Chapter 1, *Let's Understand Storm*, gets you acquainted with the problems that need distributed computing solutions. It will take you through the journey of Storm and its advent.

Chapter 2, *Getting Started with Your First Topology*, teaches you to set up the developer's environment—sandbox and execute some of the code samples.

Chapter 3, *Understanding Storm Internals by Examples*, teaches you how to prepare Storm spouts and custom spouts. You will understand various kinds of groupings provided by Storm and their application to practical problems.

Chapter 4, Storm in a Clustered Mode, teaches you how to set up a multi-node Storm cluster to get the user acquainted with the distributed Storm setup and its components. This chapter will also get your acquainted with the Storm UI and various monitoring tools for Storm.

Chapter 5, Storm High Availability and Failover, conjugates the Storm topology with the RabbitMQ broker service and explores the high availability and failover scenarios of Storm with the help of various practical examples.

Chapter 6, Adding NoSQL Persistence to Storm, introduces you to Cassandra and explores various wrapper API's available to work with Cassandra. We will use the Hector API to connect Storm and Cassandra.

Chapter 7, Cassandra Partitioning, High Availability, and Consistency, walks you through the Cassandra internals. You will understand and apply the concepts of high availability, hinted handoff, and eventual consistency in context to Cassandra.

Chapter 8, Cassandra Management and Maintenance, gets you acquainted with the management aspects of Cassandra, such as scaling the cluster, node replacement, and so on, thus equipping you with all the experience required to handle real-life situations with Cassandra.

Chapter 9, Storm Management and Maintenance, gets you acquainted with the management aspects of Storm, such as scaling the cluster, setting up parallelism, and troubleshooting Storm.

Chapter 10, Advance Concepts in Storm, gives you an understanding of the Trident API. You will be building the Trident API with certain examples and illustrations around Trident.

Chapter 11, Distributed Cache and CEP with Storm, gets you acquainted with distributed cache, its need, and applicability to solve real-life use cases with Storm. It will also educate you about Esper as a CEP in combination with Storm.

Appendix, Quiz Answers, contains all the answers to the questions of the true or false statements and the fill in the blanks section.

Bonus Chapter, Using Storm and Cassandra for Real Life Use Cases, explains a few real-life use cases and blueprints to solve these cases using the technologies such as Storm and Cassandra. This chapter can be found online at `https://www.packtpub.com/sites/default/files/downloads/Bonus_Chapter.pdf`.

What you need for this book

For this book, you will require a Linux/Ubuntu OS, Eclipse, and 8 GB of RAM. The steps to set up other components such as Storm, RabbitMQ, Cassandra, memcache, Esper, and so on are covered in chapters corresponding to the said topics.

Who this book is for

This book is intended for Java developers who wish to get started on near real-time analytics track using Storm. This will serve as an expert's guide to developing highly available and scalable solutions to complex real-time problems. Apart from development, this book also covers the management and maintenance aspects of Storm and Cassandra, which is a mandatory requirement for productionizing any solution.

Conventions

In this book, you will find a number of styles of text that distinguish between different kinds of information. Here are some examples of these styles, and an explanation of their meaning.

Code words in text, database table names, folder names, filenames, file extensions, pathnames, dummy URLs, user input, and Twitter handles are shown as follows: "The NumWorker configuration or TOPOLOGY_WORKERS configuration defined in Storm."

A block of code is set as follows:

```
// instantiates the new builder object
TopologyBuilder builder = new TopologyBuilder();
// Adds a new spout of type "RandomSentenceSpout" with a
  parallelism hint of 5
builder.setSpout("spout", new RandomSentenceSpout(), 5);
```

When we wish to draw your attention to a particular part of a code block, the relevant lines or items are highlighted:

```
public void execute(Tuple tuple) {
    String sentence = tuple.getString(0);
    for(String word: sentence.split(" ")) {
        _collector.emit(tuple, new Values(word)); //1
    }
    _collector.ack(tuple); //2
}
```

```
public void declareOutputFields(OutputFieldsDeclarer
declarer) {
    declarer.declare(new Fields("word")); //3
}
}
```

Any command-line input or output is written as follows:

```
sudo apt-get -qy install rabbitmq-server
```

New terms and **important words** are shown in bold. Words that you see on the screen, in menus or dialog boxes for example, appear in the text like this: " Go to the **Admin** tab and select **Policies** and click on **Add policy**".

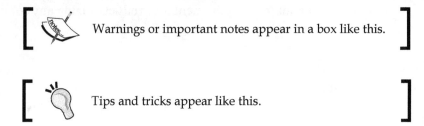

> Warnings or important notes appear in a box like this.

> Tips and tricks appear like this.

Reader feedback

Feedback from our readers is always welcome. Let us know what you think about this book—what you liked or may have disliked. Reader feedback is important for us to develop titles that you really get the most out of.

To send us general feedback, simply send an e-mail to feedback@packtpub.com, and mention the book title via the subject of your message.

If there is a topic that you have expertise in and you are interested in either writing or contributing to a book, see our author guide on www.packtpub.com/authors.

Customer support

Now that you are the proud owner of a Packt book, we have a number of things to help you to get the most from your purchase.

Downloading the example code

You can download the example code files for all Packt books you have purchased from your account at `http://www.packtpub.com`. If you purchased this book elsewhere, you can visit `http://www.packtpub.com/support` and register to have the files e-mailed directly to you.

Errata

Although we have taken every care to ensure the accuracy of our content, mistakes do happen. If you find a mistake in one of our books—maybe a mistake in the text or the code—we would be grateful if you would report this to us. By doing so, you can save other readers from frustration and help us improve subsequent versions of this book. If you find any errata, please report them by visiting `http://www.packtpub.com/submit-errata`, selecting your book, clicking on the **errata submission form** link, and entering the details of your errata. Once your errata are verified, your submission will be accepted and the errata will be uploaded on our website, or added to any list of existing errata, under the Errata section of that title. Any existing errata can be viewed by selecting your title from `http://www.packtpub.com/support`.

Piracy

Piracy of copyright material on the Internet is an ongoing problem across all media. At Packt, we take the protection of our copyright and licenses very seriously. If you come across any illegal copies of our works, in any form, on the Internet, please provide us with the location address or website name immediately so that we can pursue a remedy.

Please contact us at `copyright@packtpub.com` with a link to the suspected pirated material.

We appreciate your help in protecting our authors, and our ability to bring you valuable content.

Questions

You can contact us at `questions@packtpub.com` if you are having a problem with any aspect of the book, and we will do our best to address it.

[xi]

1
Let's Understand Storm

In this chapter, you will be acquainted with the problems requiring distributed computed solutions and get to know how complex it could get to create and manage such solutions. We will look at the options available to solve distributed computation.

The topics that will be covered in the chapter are as follows:

- Getting acquainted with a few problems that require distributed computing solutions
- The complexity of existing solutions
- Technologies offering real-time distributed computing
- A high-level view of the various components of Storm
- A quick peek into the internals of Storm

By the end of the chapter, you will be able to understand the real-time scenarios and applications of Apache Storm. You should be aware of solutions available in the market and reasons as to why Storm is still the best open source choice.

Distributed computing problems

Let's dive deep and identify some of the problems that require distributed solutions. In the world we live in today, we are so attuned to the power of now and that's the paradigm that generated the need for distributed real-time computing. Sectors such as banking, healthcare, automotive manufacturing, and so on are hubs where real-time computing can either optimize or enhance the solutions.

Real-time business solution for credit or debit card fraud detection

Let's get acquainted with the problem depicted in the following figure; when we make any transaction using plastic money and swipe our debit or credit card for payment, the duration within which the bank has to validate or reject the transaction is less than five seconds. In less than five seconds, data or transaction details have to be encrypted, travel over secure network from servicing back bank to the issuing bank, then at the issuing back bank the entire fuzzy logic for acceptance or decline of the transaction has to be computed, and the result has to travel back over the secure network:

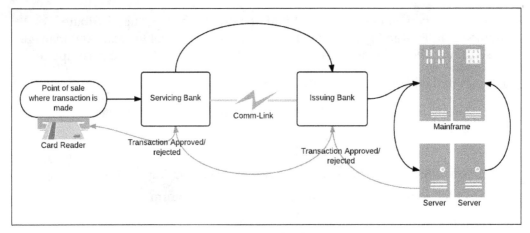

Real-time credit card fraud detection

The challenges such as network latency and delay can be optimized to some extent, but to achieve the preceding featuring transaction in less than 5 seconds, one has to design an application that is able to churn a considerable amount of data and generate results within 1 to 2 seconds.

Aircraft Communications Addressing and Reporting system

The **Aircraft Communications Addressing and Reporting** system (**ACAR**) demonstrates another typical use case that cannot be implemented without having a reliable real-time processing system in place. These Aircraft communication systems use **satellite communication** (**SATCOM**), and as per the following figure, they gather voice and packet data from all phases of flight in real time and are able to generate analytics and alerts on the data in real time.

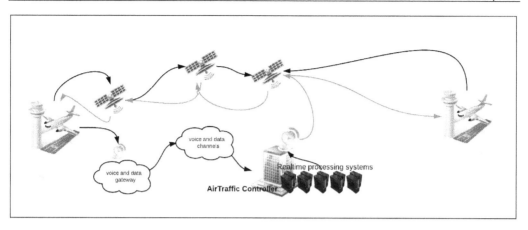

Let's take the example from the figure in the preceding case. A flight encounters some real hazardous weather, say, electric Storms on a route, then that information is sent through satellite links and voice or data gateways to the air controller, which in real time detects and raises the alerts to deviate routes for all other flights passing through that area.

Healthcare

Here, let's introduce you to another problem on healthcare.

This is another very important domain where real-time analytics over high volume and velocity data has equipped the healthcare professionals with accurate and exact information in real time to take informed life-saving actions.

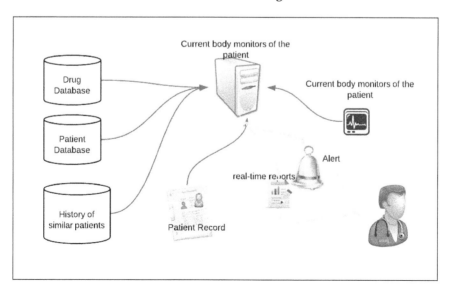

The preceding figure depicts the use case where doctors can take informed action to handle the medical situation of the patients. Data is collated from historic patient databases, drug databases, and patient records. Once the data is collected, it is processed, and live statistics and key parameters of the patient are plotted against the same collated data. This data can be used to further generate reports and alerts to aid the health care professionals.

Other applications

There are varieties of other applications where the power of real-time computing can either optimize or help people make informed decisions. It has become a great utility and aid in the following industries:

- **Manufacturing**: A real-time defect detection mechanism can help optimize production costs. Generally, in the manufacturing segment QC is performed postproduction and there, due to one similar defect in goods, entire lot is rejected.
- **Transportation industry**: Based on real-time traffic and weather data, transport companies can optimize their trade routes and save time and money.
- **Network optimization**: Based on real-time network usage alerts, companies can design auto scale up and auto scale down systems for peak and off-peak hours.

Solutions for complex distributed use cases

Now that we understand the power that real-time solutions can get into various industry verticals, let's explore and find out what options we have to process vast amount of data being generated at a very fast pace.

The Hadoop solution

The Hadoop solution is one of the solutions to solve the problems that require dealing with humongous volumes of data. It works by executing jobs in a clustered setup.

MapReduce is a programming paradigm where we process large data sets by using a mapper function that processes a key and value pair and thus generates intermediate output again in the form of a key-value pair. Then a reduce function operates on the mapper output and merges the values associated with the same intermediate key and generates a result.

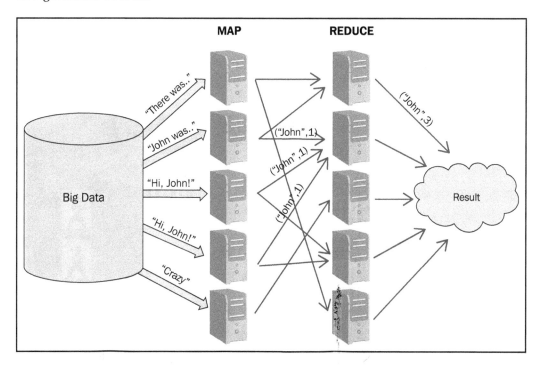

In the preceding figure, we demonstrate the simple word count MapReduce job where the simple word count job is being demonstrated using the MapReduce where:

- There is a huge Big Data store, which can go up to zettabytes or petabytes.
- Input datasets or files are split into blocks of configured size and each block is replicated onto multiple nodes in the Hadoop cluster depending upon the replication factor.
- Each mapper job counts the number of words on the data blocks allocated to it.
- Once the mapper is done, the words (which are actually the keys) and their counts are stored in a local file on the mapper node. The reducer then starts the reduce function and thus generates the result.
- Reducers combine the mapper output and the final results are generated.

Big data, as we know, did provide a solution to processing and generating results out of humongous volumes of data, but that's predominantly a batch processing system and has almost no utility on a real-time use case.

A custom solution

Here we talk about a solution that was used in the social media world before we had a scalable framework such as Storm. A simplistic version of the problem could be that you need a real-time count of the tweets by each user; Twitter solved the problem by following the mechanism shown in the figure:

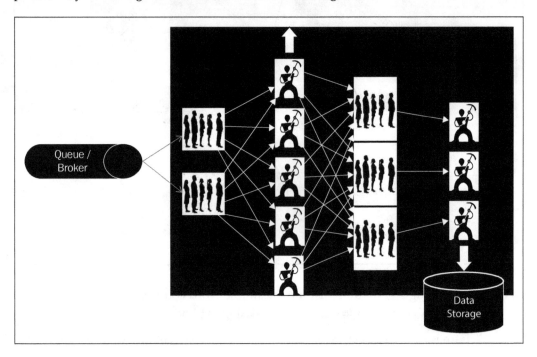

Here is the detailed information of how the preceding mechanism works:

- A custom solution created a fire hose or queue onto which all the tweets are pushed.

- A set of workers' nodes read data from the queue, parse the messages, and maintain counts of tweets by each user. The solution is scalable, as we can increase the number of workers to handle more load in the system. But the sharding algorithm for random distribution of the data among these workers nodes' should ensure equal distribution of data to all workers.

- These workers assimilate this first level count into the next set of queues.

- From these queues (the ones mentioned at level 1) second level of workers pick from these queues. Here, the data distribution among these workers is neither equal, nor random. The load balancing or the sharding logic has to ensure that tweets from the same user should always go to the same worker, to get the correct counts. For example, lets assume we have different users— "A, K, M, P, R, and L" and we have two workers "worker A" and "worker B". The tweets from user "A, K, and M" always goes to "worker A", and those of "P, R, and L users" goes to "worker B"; so the tweet counts for "A, K, and M" are always maintained by "worker A". Finally, these counts are dumped into the data store.

The queue-worker solution described in the preceding points works fine for our specific use case, but it has the following serious limitations:

- It's very complex and specific to the use case

- Redeployment and reconfiguration is a huge task

- Scaling is very tedious

- The system is not fault tolerant

Licensed proprietary solutions

After an open source Hadoop and custom Queue-worker solution, let's discuss the licensed options' proprietary solutions in the market to cater to the distributed real-time processing needs.

The **Alabama Occupational Therapy Association** (**ALOTA**) of big companies has invested in such products, because they clearly see where the future of computing is moving to. They can foresee demands of such solutions and support them in almost every vertical and domain. They have developed such solutions and products that let us do complex batch and real-time computing but that comes at a heavy license cost. A few solutions to name are from companies such as:

- **IBM**: IBM has developed InfoSphere Streams for real-time ingestion, analysis, and correlation of data.

- **Oracle**: Oracle has a product called **Real Time Decisions** (**RTD**) that provides analysis, machine learning, and predictions in real-time context

- **GigaSpaces**: GigaSpaces has come up with a product called **XAP** that provides in-memory computation to deliver real-time results

Other real-time processing tools

There are few other technologies that have some similar traits and features such as Apache Storm and S4 from Yahoo, but it lacks guaranteed processing. Spark is essentially a batch processing system with some features on micro-batching, which could be utilized as real time.

A high-level view of various components of Storm

In this section, we will get you acquainted with various components of Storm, their role, and their distribution in a Storm cluster.

A Storm cluster has three sets of nodes (which could be co-located, but are generally distributed in clusters), which are as follows:

- Nimbus
- Zookeeper
- Supervisor

The following figure shows the integration hierarchy of these nodes:

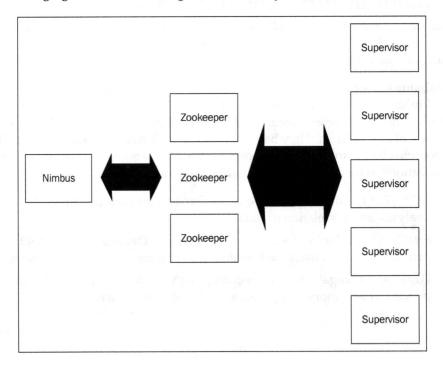

The detailed explanation of the integration hierarchy is as follows:

- **Nimbus node** (master node, similar to Hadoop-JobTracker): This is the heart of the Storm cluster. You can say that this is the master daemon process that is responsible for the following:
  - ° Uploading and distributing various tasks across the cluster
  - ° Uploading and distributing the topology jars jobs across various supervisors
  - ° Launching workers as per ports allocated on the supervisor nodes
  - ° Monitoring the topology execution and reallocating workers whenever necessary
  - ° Storm UI is also executed on the same node

- **Zookeeper nodes**: Zookeepers can be designated as the bookkeepers in the Storm cluster. Once the topology job is submitted and distributed from the Nimbus nodes, then even if Nimbus dies the topology would continue to execute because as long as Zookeepers are alive, the workable state is maintained and logged by them. The main responsibility of this component is to maintain the operational state of the cluster and restore the operational state if recovery is required from some failure. It's the coordinator for the Storm cluster.

- **Supervisor nodes**: These are the main processing chambers in the Storm topology; all the action happens in here. These are daemon processes that listen and manage the work assigned. These communicates with Nimbus through Zookeeper and starts and stops workers according to signals from Nimbus.

Delving into the internals of Storm

Now that we know which physical components are present in a Storm cluster, let's understand what happens inside various Storm components when a topology is submitted. When we say topology submission, it means that we have submitted a distributed job to Storm Nimbus for execution over the cluster of supervisors. In this section, we will explain the various steps that are executed in various Storm components when a Storm topology is executed:

- Topology is submitted on the Nimbus node.

- Nimbus uploads the code jars on all the supervisors and instructs the supervisors to launch workers as per the `NumWorker` configuration or the `TOPOLOGY_WORKERS` configuration defined in Storm.

- During the same duration all the Storm nodes (Nimbus and Supervisors) constantly co-ordinate with the Zookeeper clusters to maintain a log of workers and their activities.

As per the following figure, we have depicted the topology and distribution of the topology components, which are the same across clusters:

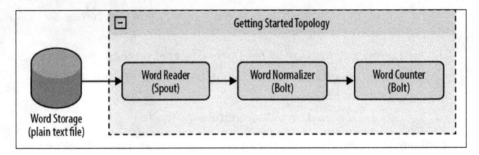

In our case, let's assume that our cluster constitutes of one Nimbus node, three Zookeepers in a Zookeeper cluster, and one supervisor node.

By default, we have four slots allocated to each supervisor, so four workers would be launched per Storm supervisor node unless the configuration is tweaked.

Let's assume that the depicted topology is allocated four workers, and it has two bolts each with a parallelism of two and one spout with a parallelism of four. So in total, we have eight tasks to be distributed across four workers.

So this is how the topology would be executed: two workers on each supervisor and two executors within each worker, as shown in the following figure:

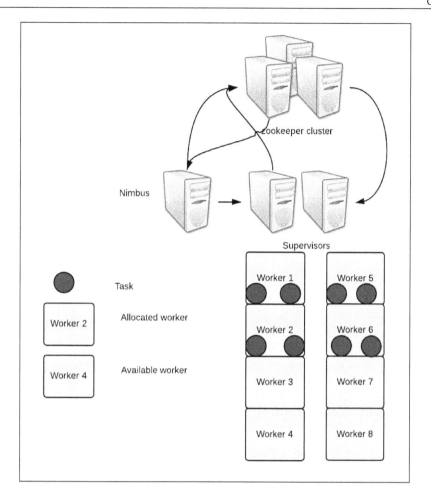

Quiz time

Q.1. Try to phrase a problem statement around real-time analytics in the following domains:

- Network optimization
- Traffic management
- Remote sensing

Summary

In this chapter, you have understood the need for distributed computing by exploring various use cases in different verticals and domains. We have also walked you through various solutions to handle these problems and why Storm is the best choice in the open source world. You have also been introduced to Storm components and the action behind the scenes when these components are at work.

In the next chapter, we will walk through the setup aspects and you will get familiarized with programming structures in Storm by simple topologies.

2
Getting Started with Your First Topology

This chapter is dedicated to guiding you through the steps to set up the environment for the execution of a Storm topology. The intent is to prepare the user sandbox and get you steered toward executing some of the sample code and understanding the working of various components. All the concepts will be accompanied by code snippets and a "try it yourself" section so that you are equipped to understand the components in a practical manner and are ready to explore and harness the power of this wonderful technology.

The topics that will be covered in this chapter are as follows:

- Storm topology and components
- Executing the sample Storm topology
- Executing the topology in distributed mode

By the end of the chapter, you will be able to understand the components and data flow in a topology, understand the simple word count topology, and execute it in the local and distributed modes. You will also be able to tweak the starter project topologies to add your own flavor to them.

Prerequisites for setting up Storm

The prerequisites for executing the setup and execution steps are enlisted here:

- For a local mode setup, you need Maven, Git, Eclipse, and Java
- For a distributed setup, you need the following:
    - A Linux or Ubuntu setup or a distributed setup can leverage PowerShell or Cygwin over their Windows systems
    - Having more than one system or virtual machines using the VMware player would help

You can refer to the following links and follow the process laid out to set up the various open source components required to set up Storm and deploy the components explained in this segment of the book:

- For Java, https://java.com/en/download/index.jsp
- For Eclipse, https://www.eclipse.org/downloads/
- For Cygwin, http://cygwin.com/install.html
- For Git, https://help.github.com/articles/set-up-git

Components of a Storm topology

A Storm topology consists of two basic components: a spout and one or more bolts. These building blocks are tied together using streams; it is over these streams that endless arrays of tuples flow.

Let's discuss the topology with a simple analogy, as depicted in the diagram and explained thereafter:

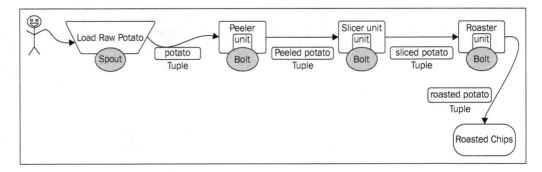

In our example topology, we have a big processing unit for roasted chips where the input, *raw potato*, is consumed by the spout, and there are various bolts such as a peeler bolt, slicer bolt, and roasting bolt that perform the tasks as their name suggests. There are various assembly lines or workers that move the chips from the peeler unit to the shredder and beyond; in our case, we have streams to link and wire in the spout and bolts with each other. Now the basic unit of exchange between the peeler and shredder is a peeled potato, and between the shredder units and roasting units is a sliced potato. This is analogous to a tuple, the datum of information exchange between spouts and bolts.

Let's take a closer look at the building blocks of the Storm topology.

 The basic unit of data interchange within Storm is called a *tuple*; this is sometimes also referred to as an *event*.

Spouts

A spout is the collection funnel of a topology; it feeds events or tuples into the topology. It can be considered as the input source to the Storm processing unit— the topology.

The spout reads messages from external sources such as a queue, file, port, and so on. Also, the spout emits them into the stream, which in turn passes them to the bolts. It's the task of the Storm spout to track each event or tuple throughout its processing through the **Directed Acyclic Graph** (**DAG**). The Storm framework then sends and generates either acknowledgement or failure notifications based on the outcome of the execution of tuples in the topology. This mechanism gives the guaranteed processing feature to Storm. Based on the required functionality, spouts can be programmed or configured to be reliable or unreliable. A reliable spout plays back the failed events into the topology.

The following diagram depicts the same flow, graphically:

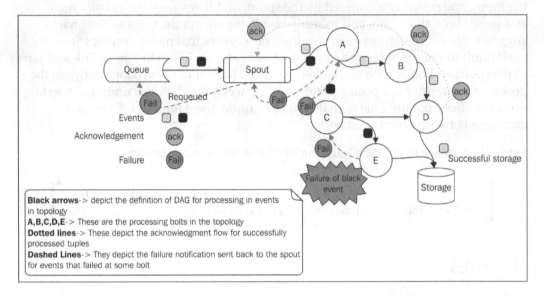

All Storm spouts are implemented to be able to emit tuples on one or more stream bolts. As in the preceding diagram, a spout can emit tuples to both bolt **A** and **C**.

Each spout should implement the **IRichSpout** interface. The following are important methods to know in context with spout:

- `nextTuple()`: This is the method that keeps on polling the external source for new events; for instance, the queue in the preceding example. On every poll, if the method finds an event, it is emitted to the topology through a stream, and if there is no new event, the method simply returns.

- `ack()`: This method is called when the tuple emitted by the spout has been successfully processed by the topology.

- `fail()`: This method is called when a tuple emitted by the spout is not successfully processed within the specified timeout. In this case, for reliable spouts, the spout traces and tracks each tuple with the `messageIds` event, which are then re-emitted to the topology to be reprocessed. For instance, in the preceding figure, the failed tuple is emitted again.

For unreliable spouts, the tuples are not tracked using `messageIds` and the methods such as `ack()` and `fail()` don't hold any value as the spout doesn't track the tuples for successful processing. These topologies are identified as unreliable.

IRichSpout is an interface provided by Storm that provides the details of the contracts or methods to be implemented by topology spouts.

Bolts

Bolts are the processing units of a topology. They are the components of the topology that perform one or more of the following tasks:

- Parsing
- Transformation
- Aggregation
- Joins
- Database interaction

The entire process being performed by the topology is generally divided into smaller tasks and subtasks, each preferably performed by a different bolt to exploit the power of the parallel distributed processing of Storm.

Let's look at the following figure that captures a real-time use case where the location coordinates from various airplanes are tracked and processed to ascertain whether they are moving on the correct trajectory:

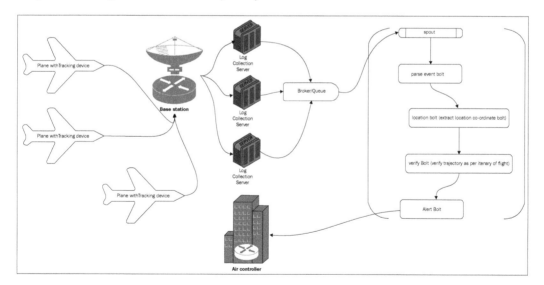

Here, the flight location coordinates are sent by sensors in the plane, which are collated at log servers and fed into a Storm topology. The Storm topology is broken into the following bolts that can act on the tuples emitted by the spout:

- **The parse event bolt**: This bolt filters and transforms the event emitted by the spout. It converts the information into a decipherable format.
- **The location bolt**: This is the bolt that extracts the location coordinates from the tuples it receives from the parse bolt and then sends them across to the next bolt.
- **The verify bolt**: This is the bolt that verifies the location coordinates sent by the location bolt against the predefined trajectory of the plane, and if it detects deviation, it sends a tuple to the alert bolt.
- **The alert bolt**: This bolt is the actor that informs the external systems, such as the air controller in our case, about the anomaly or deviation detected in the flight path.

Owing to the nature of real-time use cases, such as the one depicted in the preceding figure, speed and accuracy of computation is of utmost importance, and that's the reason that makes Storm a strong technological choice for the implementation of such solutions.

The total processing logic gets broken down into smaller tasks that are executed in bolts; configuring tasks and parallelism in bolts lets the engineers attain the right kind of performance for the solution.

One bolt can listen to multiple streams and it can emit to multiple other bolts on different streams. As depicted in the figure in the *Sprouts* section:

- Bolt-A emits to Bolt-B and Bolt-C
- Bolt-D subscribes to streams from Bolt-C and Bolt-B

The common interfaces provided by Storm to be implemented by user-defined bolts are as follows:

- IRichBolt
- IBasicBolt

The difference in these two interfaces depends upon whether reliable messaging and transactional support are required or not.

The main methods used by the bolts are as follows:

- `prepare()`: This is the method that is called when the bolt is initialized. Fundamentally, the Storm topology runs forever and the bolt once initialized will not terminate till the topology is killed. This method is generally used to initialize connections and read other static information, which is required during the entire life cycle of the bolt.

- `execute()`: This is the method that performs the functioning and processing logic defined on the bolt. It is executed for every tuple.

Streams

Stream can be defined as a sequence of tuples or events that are unbounded by nature. These streams are generally created in a parallel and distributed manner across the topology. Streams can be called the wiring or information flow channels between the spout and bolts. These are carriers of unprocessed, semiprocessed, and processed information to and from various task-performing components such as bolts and spouts. Streams are configured while encoding the topology using a schema that gives names to the fields in the stream's tuple.

Tuples – the data model in Storm

A tuple is the basic and constituent data structure in Storm. It's a named list of values that starts its journey from the spout. It's then emitted from streams to bolts, then from bolts to other bolts, where various stages of processing are executed. On successful completion of all intended processing, as per the topology definition, the tuples are acked back to the spout.

Executing a sample Storm topology – local mode

Before we start this section, the assumption is that you have gone through the prerequisites and installed the expected components.

WordCount topology from the Storm-starter project

To understand the components described in the previous section, let's download the Storm-starter project and execute a sample topology:

1. The Storm-starter project can be downloaded using the following Git command:

   ```
   Linux-command-Prompt $ sudo git clone git://github.com/apache/
   incubator-storm.git && cd incubator-storm/examples/storm-starter
   ```

2. Next, you need to import the project into your Eclipse workspace:

   1. Start Eclipse.

   2. Click on the **File** menu and select the **Import** wizard.

   3. From the **Import** wizard, select **Existing Maven Projects**.

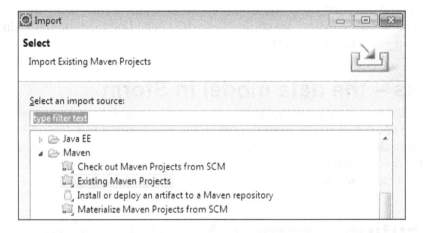

   4. Select **pom.xml** in the Storm-starter project and specify it as `<download-folder>/starter/incubator-storm/examples/storm-starter`.

   5. Once the project has been successfully imported, the Eclipse folder structure will look like the following screenshot:

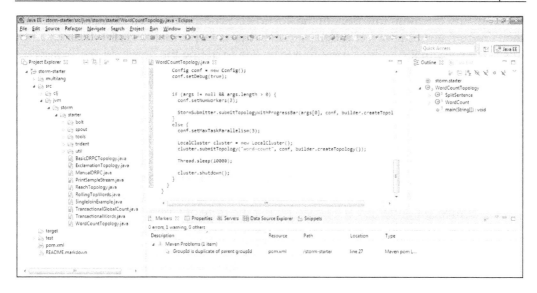

6. Execute the topology using the run command and you should be able to see the output as shown in the following screenshot:

```
11806 [Thread-33] INFO  backtype.storm.daemon.task - Emitting: split default ["keeps"]
11806 [Thread-10-count] INFO  backtype.storm.daemon.task - Emitting: count default [day, 11]
11806 [Thread-24-spout] INFO  backtype.storm.daemon.task - Emitting: spout default [four score and seven years ago]
11806 [Thread-8-count] INFO  backtype.storm.daemon.executor - Processing received message source: split:5, stream: default, id: {}, ["keeps"]
11806 [Thread-14-split] INFO  backtype.storm.daemon.executor - Processing received message source: spout:10, stream: default, id: {}, [four sco
11806 [Thread-33] INFO  backtype.storm.daemon.task - Emitting: split default ["the"]
11806 [Thread-10-count] INFO  backtype.storm.daemon.task - Emitting: count default [keeps, 11]
11807 [Thread-10-count] INFO  backtype.storm.daemon.executor - Processing received message source: split:5, stream: default, id: {}, ["the"]
11807 [Thread-33] INFO  backtype.storm.daemon.task - Emitting: split default ["doctor"]
11807 [Thread-10-count] INFO  backtype.storm.daemon.task - Emitting: count default [the, 48]
11807 [Thread-8-count] INFO  backtype.storm.daemon.executor - Processing received message source: split:5, stream: default, id: {}, ["doctor"]
11807 [Thread-33] INFO  backtype.storm.daemon.task - Emitting: split default ["away"]
11807 [Thread-8-count] INFO  backtype.storm.daemon.task - Emitting: count default [doctor, 11]
11807 [Thread-8-count] INFO  backtype.storm.daemon.executor - Processing received message source: split:5, stream: default, id: {}, ["away"]
11807 [Thread-8-count] INFO  backtype.storm.daemon.task - Emitting: count default [away, 11]
11808 [Thread-33] INFO  backtype.storm.daemon.task - Emitting: split default ["four"]
11808 [Thread-10-count] INFO  backtype.storm.daemon.executor - Processing received message source: split:5, stream: default, id: {}, ["four"]
11808 [Thread-33] INFO  backtype.storm.daemon.task - Emitting: split default ["score"]
11808 [Thread-10-count] INFO  backtype.storm.daemon.task - Emitting: count default [four, 5]
11809 [Thread-10-count] INFO  backtype.storm.daemon.executor - Processing received message source: split:5, stream: default, id: {}, ["score"]
11809 [Thread-33] INFO  backtype.storm.daemon.task - Emitting: split default ["and"]
11809 [Thread-33] INFO  backtype.storm.daemon.task - Emitting: count default [score, 5]
11809 [Thread-12-count] INFO  backtype.storm.daemon.executor - Processing received message source: split:5, stream: default, id: {}, ["and"]
11809 [Thread-33] INFO  backtype.storm.daemon.task - Emitting: split default ["seven"]
```

To understand the functioning of the topology, let's take a look at the code and understand the flow and functioning of each component in the topology:

```
// instantiates the new builder object
TopologyBuilder builder = new TopologyBuilder();
// Adds a new spout of type "RandomSentenceSpout" with a
   parallelism hint of 5
builder.setSpout("spout", new RandomSentenceSpout(), 5);
```

Starting with the main function, in the `WordCountTopology.java` class, we find the `TopologyBuilder` object called `builder`; this is important to understand as this is the class that provides us with a template to define the topology. This class exposes the API to configure and wire in various spouts and bolts into a topology — a topology that is essentially a thrift structure at the end.

In the preceding code snippet, we created a `TopologyBuilder` object and used the template to perform the following:

- `setSpout -RandomSentenceSpout`: This generates random sentences. Please note that we are using a property called parallelism hint, which is set to 5 here. This is the property that identifies how many instances of this component will be spawned at the time of submitting the topology. In our example, we will have five instances of the spout.

- `setBolt`: We use this method to add two bolts to the topology: `SplitSentenceBolt`, which splits the sentence into words, and `WordCountBolt`, which counts the words.

- Other noteworthy items in the preceding code snippet are `suffleGrouping` and `fieldsGrouping`; we shall discuss these in detail in the next chapter; for now, understand that these are the components that control routing of tuples to various bolts in the topology.

Executing the topology in the distributed mode

To set up Storm in distributed mode, we will need to perform the following steps.

Set up Zookeeper (V 3.3.5) for Storm

The coordination of a Storm topology is maintained by a Zookeeper cluster. The utilization of Zookeeper is not very high, as it just maintains the runnable state of the Storm cluster. In most cases, a single Zookeeper node should suffice, but in production scenarios, at least a three-node Zookeeper cluster is recommended so that a single node doesn't become a single point of failure.

For reliable Zookeeper service, deploy Zookeeper in a cluster known as an **ensemble**. As long as the majority of the ensemble is up, the service will be available. One of the nodes in the ensemble is automatically selected as a leader and others as followers. If the leader goes down, one of the follower nodes becomes the leader.

Perform the following steps on all the machines that will be part of the Zookeeper ensemble to set up the Zookeeper cluster:

1. Download the most recent stable release (version 3.3.5) from the Apache Zookeeper site.

2. Create a `zookeeper` directory under `/usr/local`:

    ```
    sudo mkdir /usr/local/zookeeper
    ```

3. Extract the downloaded TAR file to the `/usr/local` location. Use the following command:

    ```
    sudo tar -xvf zookeeper-3.3.5.tar.gz -C /usr/local/zookeeper
    ```

4. Zookeeper needs a directory to store its data. Create `/usr/local/zookeeper/tmp` to store this data:

    ```
    sudo mkdir -p /usr/local/zookeeper/tmp
    ```

5. Create a configuration file, `zoo.cfg`, under `/usr/local/zookeeper/zookeeper-3.3.5/conf`. The following properties will go in it:

    - `tickTime`: This is the number of milliseconds of each tick (for example, 2000).

    - `initLimit`: This is the number of ticks that the initial synchronization phase can take (for example, 5).

    - `syncLimit`: This is the number of ticks that can pass between sending a request and getting an acknowledgement (for example, 2).

    - `dataDir`: This is the directory where the snapshot is stored (for example, `/usr/local/zookeeper/tmp`).

    - `clientPort`: This is the port at which the Zookeeper clients will connect to the port (for example, 2182).

    - `server.id=host:port:port`: Every machine that is part of the Zookeeper ensemble should know about every other machine in the ensemble. This is accomplished with the series of lines of the `server.id=host:port:port` form (for example, `server.1:<IP_ADDRESS_OF_ZOOKEEPER_NODE_1>:2888:3888`).

6. Repeat the preceding steps or copy the distribution to other machines that will be part of the Zookeeper cluster.

7. Create a file with the name `myid` in the directory specified by the `datadir` property. The `myid` file consists of a single line containing only the text of that machine's ID (1 in the server and 1 in `zoo.cfg`). So, `myid` of server 1 will contain the text 1 and nothing else. The ID must be unique within the ensemble and should have a value between 1 and 255. The path of the `myid` file in this case is `vi /usr/local/zookeeper/tmp/myid`.

8. Edit the `~/.bashrc` file and add an environment variable for the Zookeeper home and add its bin directory to the `PATH` environment variable:

```
# .bashrc

# Source global definitions
if [ -f /etc/bashrc ]; then
        . /etc/bashrc
fi

# User specific aliases and functions
JAVA_HOME=/usr/lib/jvm/jdk1.6.0_25
ZOOKEEPER_HOME=/home/      /zookeeper/zookeeper-3.3.5
PATH=$PATH:$JAVA_HOME/bin:$ZOOKEEPER_HOME/bin:.

export ZOOKEEPER_HOME
export PATH
export JAVA_HOME
```

9. Source the `~/.bashrc` file after making changes. This step is required to make sure that the changes that are made to bashrc are applied to the current terminal session:

```
source ~/.bashrc
```

10. Start the Zookeeper daemon on each node by executing the following command from `$ZOOKEEPER_HOME`:

```
sudo -E bin/zkServer.sh start
```

11. Stop the Zookeeper daemon on each node by executing the following command from `$ZOOKEEPER_HOME`:

```
sudo -E bin/zkServer.sh stop
```

12. The Zookeeper status can be checked by running the following command from `$ZOOKEEPER_HOME`:

```
sudo -E bin/zkServer.sh status
```

The output for the different modes is as follows:

- If running in the standalone mode (only a single machine is part of the Zookeeper ensemble cluster), the following output will be seen on the console:

```
        mp-N155CENTOS6 datadir]$ zkServer.sh status
JMX enabled by default
Using config: /home/███/zookeeper/zookeeper-3.3.5/bin/../conf/zoo.cfg
Mode: standalone
```

- If running in the clustered mode, the following output is seen on the leader node:

```
        imp-N155CENTOS6 datadir]$ zkServer.sh status
JMX enabled by default
Using config: /home/███/zookeeper/zookeeper-3.3.5/bin/../conf/zoo.cfg
Mode: leader
```

- If running in the clustered mode, the following output is seen on the follower node:

```
        imp-N155CENTOS6 datadir]$ zkServer.sh status
JMX enabled by default
Using config: /home/███/zookeeper/zookeeper-3.3.5/bin/../conf/zoo.cfg
Mode: follower
```

By default, the Zookeeper log (`zookeeper.out`) is created at the same location from where its instance is started. This completes the Zookeeper cluster setup.

Setting up Storm in the distributed mode

Perform the following steps to set up Storm in distributed mode:

1. Download the `Storm-0.9.2-incubating.zip` package from the GitHub Storm site.

2. Create the directories `storm` and `storm/tmp` under `/usr/local`:

   ```
   sudo mkdir -p /usr/local/storm/tmp
   ```

3. Create the following directories for logs:

   ```
   sudo mkdir -p /mnt/abc_logs/storm/storm_logs
   ```

4. Extract the ZIP file on Nimbus and the worker machines from the directory at /usr/local:

```
sudo unzip -d /usr/local/storm/ storm-0.9.2 -incubating.zip
```

5. Make the following changes at /usr/local/storm/storm-0.9.2-incubating/conf/storm.yaml:

° storm.zookeeper.servers: This is a list of the hosts in the Zookeeper cluster for the Storm cluster:

```
storm.zookeeper.servers:
 "<IP_ADDRESS_OF_ZOOKEEPER_ENSEMBLE_NODE_1>"
 "<IP_ADDRESS_OF_ZOOKEEPER_ENSEMBLE_NODE_2>"
```

° storm.zookeeper.port: This is the port on which the Zookeeper cluster is running:

```
storm.zookeeper.port: 2182
```

° storm.local.dir: The Nimbus and the supervisor require a location on the local disk to store a small amount of data related to configurations and execution details of the topology. Please make sure to create the directory and assign read/write permissions on all Storm nodes. For our installation, we are going to create this directory in the /usr/local/storm/tmp location:

```
storm.local.dir: "/usr/local/storm/tmp"
```

° nimbus.host: The nodes need to know which machine is the master in order to download topology jars and confs. This property is used for this purpose:

```
nimbus.host: "<IP_ADDRESS_OF_NIMBUS_HOST>"
```

° java.library.path: This is the load path for the native libraries that Storm uses (ZeroMQ and JZMQ). The default of /usr/local/lib:/opt/local/lib:/usr/lib should be fine for most installations, so validate the libraries in the previously mentioned locations before moving forward.

° storm.messaging.netty: Storm's Netty-based transport has been overhauled to significantly improve performance through better utilization of thread, CPU, and network resources, particularly in cases where message sizes are small. In order to provide Netty support, the following configurations need to be added:

```
storm.messaging.transport:"backtype.storm.messaging.netty.
Context"
    storm.messaging.netty.server_worker_threads:1
```

```
storm.messaging.netty.client_worker_threads:1
storm.messaging.netty.buffer_size:5242880
storm.messaging.netty.max_retries:100
storm.messaging.netty.max_wait_ms:1000
storm.messaging.netty.min_wait_ms:100
```

   ° The `storm.yaml` snippet from our Storm cluster installation is
     as follows:

```
#To be filled in for a storm configuration
storm.zookeeper.servers:
    - "nim-zkp-flm-3.abc.net"
storm.zookeeper.port: 2182
storm.local.dir: "/usr/local/storm/tmp"
nimbus.host: "nim-zkp-flm-3.abc.net"
topology.message.timeout.secs: 60
topology.debug: false
topology.optimize: true
topology.ackers: 4

storm.messaging.transport: "backtype.storm.messaging.netty.
Context"
storm.messaging.netty.server_worker_threads: 1
storm.messaging.netty.client_worker_threads: 1
storm.messaging.netty.buffer_size: 5242880
storm.messaging.netty.max_retries: 100
storm.messaging.netty.max_wait_ms: 1000
storm.messaging.netty.min_wait_ms: 100
```

6. Set the `STORM_HOME` environment in the `~/.bashrc` file and add Storm's `bin`
   directory in the `PATH` environment variable. This is added to execute Storm
   binaries from any location.

7. Copy the `Storm.yaml` file to the `bin` folder of the Storm installation on the
   Nimbus machine using the following command:

```
sudo cp /usr/local/storm/storm-0.9.2-
   incubating/conf/storm.yaml /usr/local/storm/storm-0.8.2/bin/
```

Launching Storm daemons

Now that the Storm cluster is set, we will be required to start three processes on respective Storm nodes. They are as follows:

- **Nimbus:** Start Nimbus as the background process on the machine identified as the master node by running the following command from $STORM_HOME:

  ```
  sudo -bE bin/storm nimbus
  ```

- **Supervisor:** Supervisors can be started in a similar way Nimbus is started. Run the following command from $STORM_HOME:

  ```
  sudo -bE bin/storm supervisor
  ```

- **UI:** The Storm UI is a web application to check the Storm cluster, which contains the Nimbus/Supervisor status. It also lists all the running topologies and their details. The UI can be enabled by using the following command from $STORM_HOME:

  ```
  sudo -bE bin/storm ui
  ```

The UI can be accessed through http://<IP_ADDRESS_OF_NIMBUS>:8080.

Executing the topology from Command Prompt

Once the UI is visible and all the daemons are started, the topology can be submitted on Nimbus using the following command:

```
storm jar storm-starter-0.0.1-SNAPSHOT-jar-with-dependencies.jar
  storm.starter.WordCountTopology WordCount -c nimbus.host=localhost
```

The Storm UI with the WordCount topology running in distributed mode is shown here. It depicts the topology state, uptime, and other details (we shall discuss the features of the UI in detail in a later chapter). We can kill the topology from the UI.

Storm UI

Topology summary

Name	Id	Status	Uptime	Num workers	Num executors	Num tasks
WordCount	WordCount-1-1387403806	ACTIVE	6m 46s	3	28	28

Topology actions

Activate | Deactivate | Rebalance | Kill

Topology stats

Window ▲	Emitted	Transferred	Complete latency (ms)	Acked	Failed
10m 0s	241680	129620	0.000	0	0
3h 0m 0s	241680	129620	0.000	0	0
1d 0h 0m 0s	241680	129620	0.000	0	0
All time	241680	129620	0.000	0	0

Spouts (All time)

Id ▲	Executors	Tasks	Emitted	Transferred	Complete latency (ms)	Acked	Failed	Last error
spout	5	5	17540	17540	0.000	0	0	

Tweaking the WordCount topology to customize it

Now that we have deployed the WordCount topology in distributed mode, let's tweak the code in the bolts a bit to write WordCount onto a file. To achieve this, we will proceed with the following steps:

1. We intend to create a new bolt, FileWriterBolt, to achieve this. Open WordCountTopology.java and add the following snippet to WordCountTopology.java:

    ```
    public static class FileWriterBolt extends BaseBasicBolt {
        Map<String, Integer> counts = new HashMap<String,
        Integer>();
    ```

```
@Override
public void execute(Tuple tuple, BasicOutputCollector
collector) {
    String word = tuple.getString(0);
    Integer count = counts.get(word);
    if(count==null) {count = 0;
    count = 0;
}

    count++;
    counts.put(word, count);
    OutputStream ostream;
    try {
        ostream = new
        FileOutputStream("~/wordCount.txt", true);
        ostream.write(word.getBytes());
        ostream.close();
    } catch (IOException e) {
        // TODO Auto-generated catch block
        e.printStackTrace();
    }
    collector.emit(new Values(word, count));
}

@Override
public void declareOutputFields(OutputFieldsDeclarer
declarer) {
    declarer.declare(new Fields("word", "count"));
}
```

2. Next we have to make changes to the `main()` method to use this new bolt instead of `WordCount Bolt()`; here is the snippet:

```
// instantiates the new builder object
TopologyBuilder builder = new TopologyBuilder();
// Adds a new spout of type "RandomSentenceSpout" with a
  parallelism hint of 5
builder.setSpout("spout", new RandomSentenceSpout(), 5);
//Adds a new bolt to the  topology of type "SplitSentence"
  with parallelism of 8
builder.setBolt("split", new SplitSentence(),
  8).shuffleGrouping("spout");
//Adds a new bolt to the  topology of type "SplitSentence"
  with parallelism of 8
//builder.setBolt("count", new FileWriterBolt()(),
  12).fieldsGrouping("split", new Fields("word"));
```

3. Next, you can execute the topology using Eclipse, run it as Java, and the output will be saved into a file called `wordCount.txt` in your home directory.

4. To run in distributed mode, use the following steps:

   1. Compile the topology changes to generate a new Storm-starter project using the following command line:

      ```
      mvn clean install
      ```

   2. Copy `storm-starter-0.0.1-SNAPSHOT-jar-with-dependencies.jar` from the target folder under the starter project to Nimbus, let's say, at `/home/admin/topology/`.

   3. Submit the topology using the following command:

      ```
      storm jar /home/admin/topology/storm-starter-0.0.1-SNAPSHOT-
          jar-with-dependencies.jar storm.starter.WordCountTopology
          WordCount -c nimbus.host=localhost
      ```

5. The output will be the same as the `WordCount` topology executed in the figure in the preceding section.

Quiz time

Q.1. State whether the following statements are true or false:

1. All Storm topologies are reliable.
2. A topology generally has multiple spouts.
3. A topology generally has multiple bolts.
4. One bolt can emit on only one stream.

Q.2. Fill in the blanks:

1. _____ is the template to create the topology.
2. _____ specifies how many instances of a particular bolt or spout are spawned.
3. The _____ daemon of Storm is analogous to the job tracker of Hadoop.

Q.3. Perform the following task:

1. Make changes to the `WordCount` topology of the Storm-starter project to `RandomSentenceSpout` so that it's able to read sentences from a file at a specified location.

Summary

In this chapter, we have set up the Storm ensemble. You were introduced to the various building blocks of a Storm topology such as bolts, spouts, and the wiring template — topology builder. We executed and understood the `WordCount` topology and also made some amendments to it.

In the next chapter, you will read and understand about stream groupings, anchoring, and acking. That will also lead us to reliable and non-reliable mechanisms in the topologies under the Storm framework.

3
Understanding Storm
Internals by Examples

This chapter of the book is dedicated to making you understand the internals of Storm and how it works using practical examples. The intent is to get you accustomed to writing you own spouts, go through reliable and non-reliable topologies, and acquaint you with various groupings provided by the Storm.

The topics that will be covered in the chapter are as follows:

- Storm spouts and custom spouts
- Anchoring and acking
- Different stream groupings

By the end of this chapter, you should be able to understand the various groupings and the concept of reliability by using of anchoring, and you will be able to create your own spouts.

Customizing Storm spouts

You have explored and understood `WordCount` topology provided by the Storm-starter project in previous chapters. Now it's time we move on to the next step, the do it yourself journey with Storm; so let's take up the next leap and do some exciting stuff with our own spouts that read from various sources.

Creating FileSpout

Here we will create our own spout to read the events or tuples from a file source and emit them into the topology; we would substitute spout in place of RandomSentenceSpout we used in the WordCount topology in the previous chapter.

To start, copy the project we created in *Chapter 2, Getting Started with Your First Topology*, into a new project and make the following changes in RandomSentenceSpout to make a new class called FileSpout within the Storm-starter project.

Now we will make changes in FileSpout so that it reads sentences from a file as shown in the following code:

```
public class FileSpout extends BaseRichSpout {
  //declaration section
  SpoutOutputCollector _collector;
  DataInputStream in ;
  BufferedReader br;
  Queue qe;

  //constructor
    public FileSpout() {
        qe = new LinkedList();
    }

  // the messageId builder method
  private String getMsgId(int i) {
    return (new StringBuilder("#@#MsgId")).append(i).toString();
    }

  //The function that is called at every line being read by
  readFile
  //method and adds messageId at the end of each line and then add
  // the line to the linked list
    private void queueIt() {
      int msgId = 0;
      String strLine;
      try {
          while ((strLine = br.readLine()) != null) {
              qe.add((new
              StringBuilder(String.valueOf(strLine))).append("#@#"
              + getMsgId(msgId)).toString());
              msgId++;
          }
      } catch (IOException e) {
```

```
            e.printStackTrace();
        } catch (Exception e) {
            e.printStackTrace();
        }
    }


//function to read line from file at specified location
private void readFile() {
        try {
            FileInputStream fstream = new
            FileInputStream("/home/mylog"); in =
            new DataInputStream(fstream);
            br = new BufferedReader(new InputStreamReader( in ));
            queueIt();
            System.out.println("FileSpout file reading done");
        } catch (FileNotFoundException e) {
            e.printStackTrace();
        }
    }


//open function that is called at the time of spout
initialization
// it calls the readFile method that reads the file , adds
events
// to the linked list to be fed to the spout as tuples
@
  Override
  public void open(Map conf, TopologyContext context,
  SpoutOutputCollector
  collector) {
    _collector = collector;
    readFile();
  }


//this method is called every 100 ms and it polls the list
//for message which is read off as next tuple and emit the spout
to
//the topology. When queue doesn't have any events, it reads the
//file again calling the readFile method
  @
  Override
  public void nextTuple() {
    Utils.sleep(100);
    String fullMsg = (String) qe.poll();
```

```
        String msg[] = (String[]) null;
        if (fullMsg != null) {
            msg = (new String(fullMsg)).split("#@#");
            _collector.emit(new Values(msg[0]));
            System.out.println((new StringBuilder("nextTuple done
            ")).append(msg[1]).toString());
        } else {
            readFile();
        }
    }


    @
    Override
    public void ack(Object id) {}


    @
    Override
    public void fail(Object id) {}


    @
    Override
    public void declareOutputFields(OutputFieldsDeclarer declarer) {
        declarer.declare(new Fields("word"));
    }
}
```

Tweaking WordCount topology to use FileSpout

Now we need to fit FileSpout into our WordCount topology and execute it. To do this, you need to change one line of code in WordCount topology and instantiate FileSpout instead of RandomSentenceSpout in TopologyBuilder, as shown here:

```
public static void main(String[] args) throws Exception {
    TopologyBuilder builder = new TopologyBuilder();
//builder.setSpout("spout", new RandomSentenceSpout(), 5);
    builder.setSpout("spout", new FileSpout(), 1);
```

This one line change will take care of instantiation of the new spout that will read from the specified file /home/mylog (please create this file before you execute the program). Here is a screenshot of the output for your reference:

```
<terminated> WordCountTopology [Java Application] /usr/lib/jvm/jdk1.7.0_45/bin/java (13-Aug-2014 12:27:32 am)
9145 [Thread-8-count] INFO  backtype.storm.daemon.executor - Processing received message source: split:5, stream: default, id: {}, ["jumped"]
9146 [Thread-8-count] INFO  backtype.storm.daemon.task - Emitting: count default [jumped, 8]
9146 [Thread-19] INFO  backtype.storm.daemon.task - Emitting: split default ["over"]
9147 [Thread-19] INFO  backtype.storm.daemon.task - Emitting: split default ["the"]
9147 [Thread-10-count] INFO  backtype.storm.daemon.executor - Processing received message source: split:5, stream: default, id: {}, ["over"]
9147 [Thread-10-count] INFO  backtype.storm.daemon.task - Emitting: count default [over, 8]
9148 [Thread-10-count] INFO  backtype.storm.daemon.executor - Processing received message source: split:5, stream: default, id: {}, ["the"]
9148 [Thread-10-count] INFO  backtype.storm.daemon.task - Emitting: count default [the, 16]
9148 [Thread-19] INFO  backtype.storm.daemon.task - Emitting: split default ["moon"]
9148 [Thread-10-count] INFO  backtype.storm.daemon.executor - Processing received message source: split:5, stream: default, id: {}, ["moon"]
9148 [Thread-10-count] INFO  backtype.storm.daemon.task - Emitting: count default [moon, 8]
FileSpout file reading done
9344 [Thread-24-spout] INFO  backtype.storm.daemon.task - Emitting: spout default [the cow jumped over the moon]
nextTuple done MsgId0
9345 [Thread-18-split] INFO  backtype.storm.daemon.executor - Processing received message source: spout:8, stream: default, id: {}, [the cow jumped o
9346 [Thread-27] INFO  backtype.storm.daemon.task - Emitting: split default ["the"]
9348 [Thread-10-count] INFO  backtype.storm.daemon.executor - Processing received message source: split:7, stream: default, id: {}, ["the"]
9348 [Thread-10-count] INFO  backtype.storm.daemon.task - Emitting: count default [the, 17]
9348 [Thread-27] INFO  backtype.storm.daemon.task - Emitting: split default ["cow"]
9350 [Thread-8-count] INFO  backtype.storm.daemon.executor - Processing received message source: split:7, stream: default, id: {}, ["cow"]
9351 [Thread-8-count] INFO  backtype.storm.daemon.task - Emitting: count default [cow, 9]
9351 [Thread-27] INFO  backtype.storm.daemon.task - Emitting: split default ["jumped"]
9353 [Thread-27] INFO  backtype.storm.daemon.task - Emitting: split default ["over"]
9353 [Thread-8-count] INFO  backtype.storm.daemon.executor - Processing received message source: split:7, stream: default, id: {}, ["jumped"]
9354 [Thread-8-count] INFO  backtype.storm.daemon.task - Emitting: count default [jumped, 9]
9354 [Thread-10-count] INFO  backtype.storm.daemon.executor - Processing received message source: split:7, stream: default, id: {}, ["over"]
9355 [Thread-27] INFO  backtype.storm.daemon.task - Emitting: split default ["the"]
9355 [Thread-10-count] INFO  backtype.storm.daemon.task - Emitting: count default [over, 9]
9356 [Thread-10-count] INFO  backtype.storm.daemon.executor - Processing received message source: split:7, stream: default, id: {}, ["the"]
9356 [Thread-10-count] INFO  backtype.storm.daemon.task - Emitting: count default [the, 18]
9356 [Thread-27] INFO  backtype.storm.daemon.task - Emitting: split default ["moon"]
9357 [Thread-10-count] INFO  backtype.storm.daemon.executor - Processing received message source: split:7, stream: default, id: {}, ["moon"]
9358 [Thread-10-count] INFO  backtype.storm.daemon.task - Emitting: count default [moon, 9]
```

The count is being increased as the same sentence is being emitted the cow jumped over again from the file spout

The SocketSpout class

As a next step to understand the spouts better, let's create a SocketSpout class. Assuming that you are proficient in writing Socket Server or Producer, I will walk you through the process of creating a custom SocketSpout class to consume a socket output in the Storm topology:

```
public class SocketSpout extends BaseRichSpout{
  static SpoutOutputCollector collector;
  //The socket
    static Socket myclientSocket;
    static ServerSocket myserverSocket;
    static int myport;

  public SocketSpout(int port){
    myport=port;
  }

  public void open(Map conf,TopologyContext context,
  SpoutOutputCollector collector){
    _collector=collector;
    myserverSocket=new ServerSocket(myport);
  }
```

```
public void nextTuple(){
  myclientSocket=myserverSocket.accept();
  InputStream incomingIS=myclientSocket.getInputStream();
  byte[] b=new byte[8196];
  int len=b.incomingIS.read(b);
  _collector.emit(new Values(b));
  }
}
```

Anchoring and acking

We have talked about DAG that is created for the execution of a Storm topology. Now when you are designing your topologies to cater to reliability, there are two items that needs to be added to Storm:

- Whenever a new link, that is, a new stream is being added to the DAG, it is called anchoring
- When the tuple is processed in entirety, it is called acking

When Storm knows these preceding facts, then during the processing of tuples it can gauge them and accordingly fail or acknowledge the tuples depending upon whether they are completely processed or not.

Let's take a look at the following WordCount topology bolts to understand the Storm API anchoring and acking better:

- SplitSentenceBolt: The purpose of this bolt was to split the sentence into different words and emit it. Now let's examine the output declarer and the execute methods of this bolt in detail (specially the highlighted sections) as shown in the following code:

```
public void execute(Tuple tuple) {
    String sentence = tuple.getString(0);
    for(String word: sentence.split(" ")) {
        _collector.emit(tuple, new Values(word)); //1
    }
    _collector.ack(tuple); //2
}
public void declareOutputFields(OutputFieldsDeclarer
declarer) {
    declarer.declare(new Fields("word")); //3
}
}
```

The output declarer functionality of the preceding code is elaborated as follows:

- `_collector.emit`: Here each tuple being emitted by the bolt on the stream called `word` (the second argument) is anchored using the first argument of the method (the tuple). In this arrangement, if a failure occurs the tuple being anchored at the root of the tree would be replayed by the spout.

- `collector.ack`: Here we are informing Storm that tuple has been processed successfully by this bolt. In the event of a failure, the programmer can explicitly call a `fail` method, or Storm internally calls it, as in the case of timeout events so that it can be replayed.

- `declarer.declare`: This is the method called to specify the stream on which successfully processed tuples would be emitted. Notice that we have used the same `word` stream in the `_collector.emit` method. Similarly, if you look into the `WordCount` topology's `Builder` method, you'd find another piece in overall integration of `word` stream, which is as follows:

  ```
  builder.setBolt("count", new WordCount(),
  12).fieldsGrouping("split", new Fields("word"));
  ```

The unreliable topology

Now let's look at the unreliable version of the same topology. Here, if the tuple fails to be processed by Storm in entirety, it is not replayed by the framework. The code which we used previously, in this topology, would look like this:

```
java _collector.emit(new Values(word));
```

Thus, an un-anchored tuple is emitted by the bolt. Sometimes, due to programming needs to handle various problems, developers deliberately create unreliable topologies.

Stream groupings

Next we need to get acquainted with various stream groupings (a stream grouping is basically the mechanism that defines how Storm partitions and distributes the streams of tuples amongst tasks of bolts) provided by Storm. Streams are the basic wiring component of a Storm topology, and understanding them provides a lot of flexibility to the developer to handle various problems in programs efficiently.

Local or shuffle grouping

Local or shuffle grouping is the most common grouping that randomly distributes the tuples emitted by the source ensuring equal distribution, that is, each instance of the bolt gets to process the same number of events. Load balancing is automatically taken care of by this grouping.

Due to the random nature of distribution of this grouping, it's useful only for atomic operations by specifying a single parameter—source of stream. The following snippet is from WordCount topology (which we reated earlier), which demonstrates the usage of shuffle grouping:

```
TopologyBuilder myBuilder = new TopologyBuilder();
builder.setSpout("spout", new RandomSentenceSpout(), 5);
builder.setBolt("split", new SplitSentence(),
   8).shuffleGrouping("spout");
builder.setBolt("count", new WordCount(),
   12).fieldsGrouping("split", new Fields("word"));
```

In the following figure, shuffle grouping is depicted:

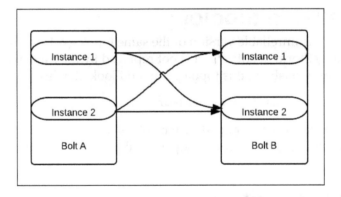

Here **Bolt A** and **Bolt B** both have a parallelism of two, each; so two instances of each of these bolts is spawned by the Storm framework. These bolts are wired together by *shuffle grouping*. We will now discuss the distribution of events.

The 50 percent events from **Instance 1** of **Bolt A** would go to **Instance 1** of **Bolt B**, and the remaining 50 percent would go to **Instance 2** of **Bolt B**. Similarly, 50 percent of events emitted by **Instance 2** of **Bolt B** would go to **Instance 1** of **Bolt B**, and the remaining 50 percent would go to **Instance 2** of **Bolt B**.

Fields grouping

In this grouping, we specify two parameters — the source of the stream and the fields. The values of the fields are actually used to control the routing of the tuples to various bolts. This grouping guarantees that for the same field's value, the tuple will always be routed to the same instance of the bolt.

In the following figure, field grouping is depicted between **Bolt A** and **Bolt B**, and each of these bolts have two instances each. Notice the flow of events based on the value of the field grouping parameter.

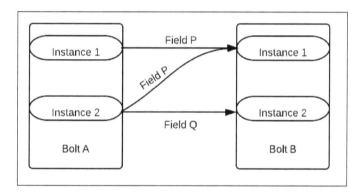

All the events from **Instance 1** and **Instance 2** of **Bolt A**, where the value of **Field** is P are sent to **Instance 1** of **Bolt B**.

All the events from **Instance 1** and **Instance 2** of **Bolt A**, where the value of **Field** is Q are sent to **Instance 2** of **Bolt B**.

All grouping

All grouping is a kind of broadcaster grouping that can be used in situations where the same message needs to be sent to all instances of the destination bolt. Here, each tuple is sent to all the instances of the bolt.

This grouping should be used in very specific cases, for specific streams, where we want the same information to be replicated to all bolt instances downstream. Let's take a use case that has some information related to a country and its currency value and the bolts following the bolt, which does need this information for some currency conversion. Now whenever *currency* bolt has any changes, it uses *all* grouping to publish it to all the instances of the following bolts:

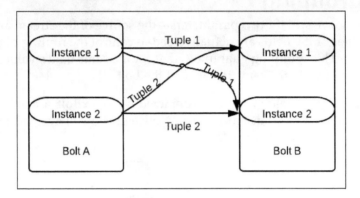

Here we have a diagrammatic representation of *all* grouping, where all the tuples from **Bolt A** are sent to all the instances of **Bolt B**.

Global grouping

Global grouping makes sure that the entire stream from the source component (spout or bolt) goes to a single instance of target bolt, to be more precise and specific to the instance of the target bolt with the lowest ID. Well let's understand the concept with an example, let's say my topology is as follows:

mySpout → myboltA → myboltB

I will assign the following parallelism to the components:

mySpout (2) → myboltA (3) → myboltB (2)

Also, I will use the following stream groupings:

mySpout (2) →(shuffle grouping)→myboltA (3)→ (global grouping)→myboltB (2)

Then, the framework will direct all data from the *myboltA* stream instances, that are emitting onto one instance of *myboltB* stream, which would be the one to which Storm has assigned a lower ID while instantiation:

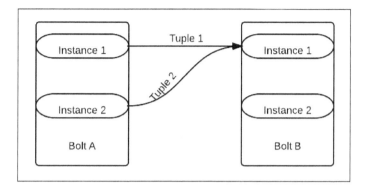

As in the preceding figure, in the case of global grouping, all tuples from both instances of **Bolt A** would go to **Instance 1** of **Bolt B**, assuming it has a lower ID than **Instance 2** of **Bolt B**.

 Storm basically assigns IDs to each instance of a bolt or spout that it creates in the topology. In global grouping, the allocations are directed to the instance that has a lower value on the ID allocated from Storm.

Custom grouping

Storm, being an extendible framework, provides the facility to developers to create their own stream grouping. This can be done by providing an implementation to the `backtype.storm.grouping.CustomStreamGroupinginterface` class.

Direct grouping

In this kind of grouping, the Storm framework provides the ability to the sender

component (spout or bolt) to decide which task of the consumer bolt would receive the tuple while the sender component is emitting a tuple to the stream.

The tuple must be emitted to the stream using a special `emitDirect` method to the stream, and the task of consuming a component has to be specified (note that the tasked can be fetched using the `TopologyContext` method).

Quiz time

Q.1 State whether the following statements are true or false:

1. All components of reliable topologies use anchoring.
2. In the event of a failure, all the tuples are played back again.
3. Shuffle grouping does load balancing.
4. Global grouping is like a broadcaster.

Q.2 Fill in the blanks:

1. _____ is the method to tell the framework that the tuple has been successfully processed.
2. The _____ method specifies the name of the stream.
3. The _____ method is used to push the tuple downstream in the DAG.

Make changes to WordCount topology of the Storm-starter project to create a custom grouping so that all words starting from a particular letter always go to same instance of the WordCount bolt.

Summary

In this chapter, we have understood the intricacies of the Storm spout. We also created a custom file spout and integrated it with WordCount topology. We also introduced you to the concepts of reliability, acking, and anchoring. The knowledge of various groupings provided by the current version of Storm further enhance the capabilities of a user to explore and experiment.

In the next chapter, we shall get you acquainted with the clustered setup of Storm as well as give you an insight on various monitoring tools of clustered mode.

Storm in a Clustered Mode

We have now arrived at the next step in our journey with Storm, that is, to understand the clustered mode setup of Storm and its associated components. We will go through the various configurations in Storm and Zookeeper, and understand the concepts behind them.

The topics that will be covered in this chapter are as follows:

- Setting up the Storm cluster
- Understanding the configuration of the cluster and its impact on the functioning of the system
- The Storm UI and understanding the UI parameters
- Provisioning and monitoring applications for production setups

By the end of the chapter, you should be able to understand configurations of Storm and Zookeeper nodes. Also, you should be able to understand the Storm UI and set up Storm clusters and monitor them using various tools.

The Storm cluster setup

Depicted in the following figure is the Storm and Zookeeper reference cluster that we set up in *Chapter 2*, *Getting Started with Your First Topology*.

We have three-node Zookeeper clusters for a three-node Storm cluster (which has one Nimbus and two supervisors).

We are using the recommended three-node Zookeeper clusters to avoid a single point of failure in the Storm set up.

The Zookeeper cluster should have an odd number of nodes. The reason for this requirement is that the Zookeeper election logic requires the leader to have an odd number of votes, and that combination is possible only when odd nodes are in the quorum, as shown in the following figure:

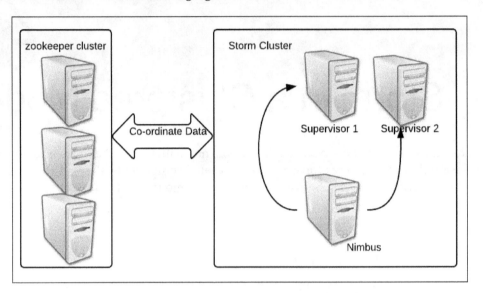

Zookeeper configurations

Let's assume you have installed Zookeeper on all three Zookeeper nodes; now we will walk you through the configurations so that you have a better understanding of them.

An excerpt from `zoo.cfg`, in our case, is located at `<zookeeper_installation_dir>/ zookeeper-3.4.5/conf/`. The Zookeeper configurations are as follows:

- `dataDir=/usr/local/zookeeper/tmp`: This is the path where Zookeeper stores its snapshots; these snapshots are actually the state log where the current cluster state is maintained for the purpose of coordination. In the event of a failure, these snapshots are used to restore the cluster to the last stable state. This directory also contains a file containing a single entry called `myID`. This value starts from 1 and is different for each Zookeeper node, so we will keep it as follows:

  ```
  zkp-1.mydomain.net - value of myId =1
  zkp-2.mydomain.net - value of myId =2
  zkp-3.mydomain.net - value of myId =3
  ```

Whenever you want to start from scratch, or when you upscale or downscale Storm or Zookeeper clusters, it is recommended that you clean up this `local.dir` file so that stale data is cleared.

- `clientPort=2182`: This configuration specifies the port on which the clients build connections with Zookeeper:

```
server.1=zkp-1.mydomain.net:2888:3888
server.2=zkp-2. mydomain.net:2888:3888
server.3=zkp-3. mydomain.net:2888:3888
```

These three rows in the preceding code actually specify the IP or the names of the servers that form a part of the Zookeeper cluster. In this configuration, we have created the three-node Zookeeper cluster.

- `maxClientCnxns=301`: This number specifies the maximum number of connections a single client can make with this Zookeeper node. Here is how the calculation will go in our case:

The max number of connections one supervisor can make is 30 with one Zookeeper node. So, the maximum number of connections one supervisor can create with three Zookeeper nodes is 90 (that is, 30*3).

The following screenshot shows a capture from the Storm UI depicting the used, available, and free slots:

 The number of workers in the Storm cluster is related to the number of connections available in the Zookeeper cluster. If you don't have sufficient Zookeeper cluster connections, Storm supervisors will not be able to start.

Cleaning up Zookeeper

We have seen how Zookeeper stores all its coordination data in the form of snapshots in the path specified in the `dataDir` configuration. This requires periodic clean up or archival to remove old snapshots so that we don't end up consuming the entire disk space. Here is a small cleanup script that needs to be configured on all Zookeeper nodes:

```
numBackUps=3
dataDir=/usr/local/zookeeper/tmp
```

```
logDir=/mnt/my_logs/
echo `date`' Time to clean up StormZkTxn logs' >>
    $logDir/cleanStormZk.out
java -cp /usr/local/zookeeper/zookeeper-3.4.5/zookeeper-
    3.4.5.jar:/usr/local/zookeeper/zookeeper-3.4.5/lib/log4j-
    1.2.15.jar:/usr/local/zookeeper/zookeeper-3.4.5/lib/slf4j-api-
    1.6.1.jar org.apache.zookeeper.server.PurgeTxnLog $dataDir -n
    $numBackUps >> $logDir/cleanStormZk.out
```

Here we have the cleanup script as follows:

- numBackUps: Here we specify how many snapshots we want to retain after cleanup; the minimum is three and the maximum can vary as per requirements.

- dataDir: Here we specify the path of the data directory where snapshots need to be cleaned up.

- logDir: This is the path where the clean up script will store its logs.

- org.apache.zookeeper.server.PurgeTxnLog: This is the utility class that purges all snapshots except the last three, as mentioned in numBackups.

Storm configurations

We will look at the Storm daemons and configurations around the daemons.
For the Nimbus node, we have the following configuration settings in storm.yaml.
Let's understand these configurations as given in the following code:

```
storm.zookeeper.servers:
- "zkp-1.mydomain.net "
- "zkp-2.mydomain.net "
- "zkp-3.mydomain.net "

storm.zookeeper.port: 2182
storm.local.dir: "/usr/local/storm/tmp"
nimbus.host: "nim-zkp-flm-3.mydomain.net"
topology.message.timeout.secs: 60
topology.debug: false

supervisor.slots.ports:
    - 6700
    - 6701
    - 6702
    - 6703
```

The functions of the configurations used in the preceding code are as follows:

- `storm.zookeeper.servers`: Here we specify the names or IPs of the Zookeeper servers from the Zookeeper cluster; note that we are using the same host names as mentioned in the `zoo.cfg` configuration in the previous section.

- `storm.zookeeper.port`: Here we specify the port on the Zookeeper node to which the Storm nodes connect. Again, we specified the same port that we had specified on `zoo.cfg` in the previous section.

- `storm.local.dir`: Storm has its own temporary data that is stored in a local directory. This data is automatically cleaned up, but whenever you want to start from scratch, or when you upscale or downscale the Storm or Zookeeper clusters, it is recommended that you clean up this `local.dir` configuration so that stale data is cleared.

- `nimbus.host`: This specifies the hostname or IP of the hostname that is being set as Nimbus.

- `topology.message.timeout.secs`: This value specifies the duration in seconds after which a tuple being processed by the topology is declared as timed out and discarded. Thereafter, depending upon whether it's a reliable or unreliable topology, it's replayed or not. This value should be set cautiously; if set too low, all messages will end up being timed out. If it is set too high, one may never get to know the performance bottlenecks in the topology.

- `topology.debug`: This parameter denotes whether you want to run the topology in the debug mode or node. The debug mode is when all the debug logs are printed, and it is recommended in the development and staging mode, but not in the production mode because I/O is very high in this mode and thus hits the overall performance.

- `supervisor.slots.ports`: This parameter specifies the ports for the supervisor workers. This number directly ties to the number of workers that can be spawned on the supervisor. When topologies are spawned, one has to specify the number of workers that are to be allocated, which in turn ties to actual resources allocated to the topology. The number of workers is really important because they actually identify how many topologies can run on the cluster and in turn how much parallelism can be achieved. For example, by default, we have four slots per supervisor, so in our cluster, we will have *Total number of slots/workers = 4*2 = 8*. Each worker takes a certain number of resources from the system in terms of CPU and RAM, so how many workers are spawned on the supervisor depends on the system configuration.

Storm logging configurations

Now we will have a look at the logging configurations of Storm. They use the `logback` implementation of Log4J and its configurations can be found and tweaked from `cluster.xml` located at `<storm-installation-dir>/apache-storm-0.9.2-incubating/logback` using the following code:

```
<appender name="A1"
    class="ch.qos.logback.core.rolling.RollingFileAppender">
    <file>${storm.log.dir}/${logfile.name}</file>
    <rollingPolicy
    class="ch.qos.logback.core.rolling.FixedWindowRollingPolicy">
      <fileNamePattern>${storm.log.dir}/${logfile.name}.%i</
fileNamePattern
      >
      <minIndex>1</minIndex>
      <maxIndex>9</maxIndex>
    </rollingPolicy>

    <triggeringPolicy
    class="ch.qos.logback.core.rolling.SizeBasedTriggeringPolicy">
      <maxFileSize>100MB</maxFileSize>
    </triggeringPolicy>

    <encoder>
      <pattern>%d{yyyy-MM-dd HH:mm:ss} %c{1} [%p] %m%n</pattern>
    </encoder>
  </appender>

  <root level="INFO">
    <appender-ref ref="A1"/>
  </root>
```

In the preceding snippet, a few sections are highlighted, which we will walk through for a closer look. They are as follows:

- `<file>`: This tag holds the log directory path and the filename on which the logs are generated by the Storm framework.

- `<filenamepattern>`: This is the pattern in which files are formed and rolled over; for example, with the preceding code pattern, we have worker log files as `worker-6700.log` and `worker-6700.1.log`.

- `<minIndex>` and `<maxIndex>`: These are very important in order to specify how many files we want to retain with this rolling appender; in this case, we will have nine backup files, which are numbered from one to nine, and one running log file.

- `maxFileSize`: This parameter specifies at what size the file should rollover, for instance, in our case, it's 100 MB; this means the worker log file will roll over to the next index when it reaches this size.

- `root level`: This specifies the logging level; in our case, we have specified it as *Info*, which means `Info` and the above logs will be printed in the log files, but logs from levels below the `Info` level will not be written to the logs. The following is the logging level hierarchy for reference:
    - OFF
    - FATAL
    - ERROR
    - WARN
    - INFO
    - DEBUG
    - TRACE
    - ALL

The Storm UI

Storm provides a UI that can be accessed to check various parameters in the Storm configuration and topology metrics. In this section, we will understand the various components of the Storm UI.

The following screenshot depicts the landing page of the Storm UI. The details of various sections are captured in the figure itself:

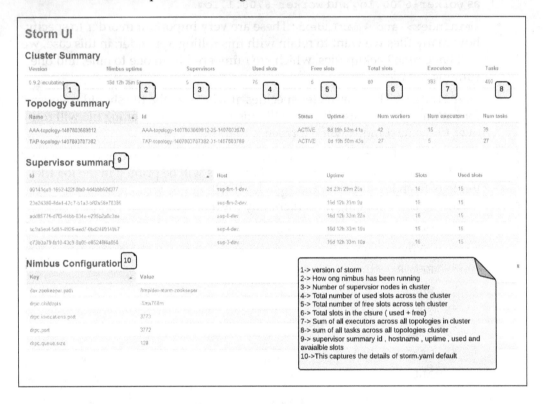

The following screenshot is a deeper look at the Storm UI; here we are looking at the UI projection for a particular topology:

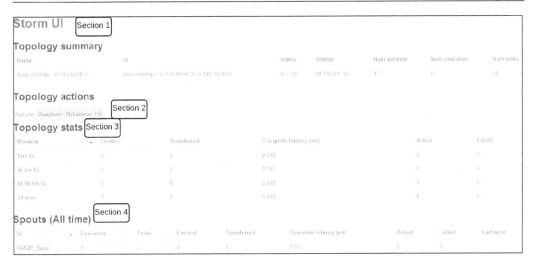

I have demarcated sections on the preceding screenshot; let's discuss them in detail so that you understand each of them completely.

Section 1

This section holds the summary of the topologies running in the Storm cluster. Here are details of various attributes captured in this section:

- **Topology Name**: This is specified when submitting the topology. You can refer to the WordCountTopology.java file, which we created earlier. The following snippet, word-count, is the name of that topology:

```
cluster.submitTopology("word-count", conf,
    builder.createTopology());
```

In our preceding sample screenshot, **AAA-topology-1407803669812** is the name of the topology.

- **ID**: This is the Storm-generated unique ID that is a combination of the topology name, timestamp, and ID, which is used by Storm to identify and differentiate the topology.

- **Status**: This denotes the state of the topology, which could be *active* for a live topology, *killed* when a topology is killed using the UI or CLI, *inactive* for a deactivated topology, and *rebalancing* for a topology where the rebalance command is executed wherein the number of workers allocated to the topology is increased or decreased.

- **Uptime**: As the name suggests, this mentions the duration for which the topology has been running. For example, our sample topology has been running for 8 days 15 hours 6 months 16 seconds.

- **Num workers**: This specifies how many workers are allocated to the topology. Again, if we refer to `WordCountTopology.java`, we will see this snippet where it is declared as 3:

```
conf.setNumWorkers(3);
```

- **Num executors**: This specifies the sum total of the number of executors in the topology. This is connected to the parallelism hint that is specified during the overall integration of the topology in the topology builder as follows:

```
builder.setSpout("spout", new RandomSentenceSpout(), 5);
```

Here, in our `WordCount` topology, we have specified the parallelism of the spout as 5, so five instances of the spout will be spawned in the topology.

- **Num tasks**: This gains the sum total of another parameter that is specified at the time of overall integration in the topology, as shown:

```
builder.setSpout("spout", new RandomSentenceSpout(),
    5).setNumTasks(10);
```

Here, we are specifying that for 5 executors dedicated to the spout, the total value of `numtasks` is 10, so two tasks each will be spawned on each of the executors.

What we see on the UI is a total of all `numtasks` values across all topology components.

Section 2

This section holds the various actions that can be performed on the topology:

- **Activate**: The UI provides a facility to revive or reactivate a topology that has been suspended earlier. Once activated, it can again start consuming the messages from the spout and process them.

- **Deactivate**: When this action is executed, the topology immediately turns off the spout, that is, no new messages are read from the spout and pushed downstream to the DAG. Existing messages that are already being processed in various bolts are processed completely.

- **Rebalance**: This action is executed when the worker allocation to a live topology is altered.

- **Kill**: As the name suggests, this is used to send a termination signal for the topology to the Storm framework. It's always advisable to provide a reasonable kill time so that the topology drains completely and is able to clean the pipelined events before it terminates.

Section 3

This section displays a capture of the number of messages processed on the timeline. It has the following key sections:

- **Window**: This field specifies the time duration in the following segments: last for 10 minutes, last 3 hours, the past day, or all the time. The topology's progress is captured against these time sections.
- **Emitted**: This captures the number of tuples emitted by the spout at various time segments.
- **Transferred**: This specifies the number of tuples sent to other components in the topology. Please note that the number of emitted tuples may or may not be equal to the number of transferred tuples as the former is the exact number of times the emit method of the spout is executed, while the latter is the number transferred based on the grouping used; for example, if we have bound a spout to a bolt that has the parallelism of two tuples using all grouping, then for every x tuples emitted by the spout, 2x tuples will be transferred.
- **Complete latency(ms)**: This is the average total time taken by a tuple to execute throughout the topology.
- **Acked**: This holds the number of events acked that are successfully processed.
- **Failed**: This is the number of events that failed to process successfully.

Section 4

This section is the same as *Section 3*, the only difference being that here, the terms are displayed at a component level, that is spouts and bolts, while in *Section 3*, it was at the topology level. There are a few more terms on the UI that you should be introduced to. They are as follows:

- **Capacity**: This is one of the most important metrics to look at when fine-tuning the topology. It indicates the percentage of time the bolt spent in the last ten minutes to execute the tuple. Any value close to one or above is an indication to increase the parallelism of this bolt. It's calculated using the following formula:

```
Capacity = (Number of tuples Executed*Average execute
    latency)/Window_Size*1000)
```

- **Execute latency**: This is the average time a tuple spends in the execute method of the bolt during processing.

- **Process latency**: Process latency is the average time it takes from when the tuple is received by the bolt to the time when it's acked (acknowledged to denote successful processing).

The visualization section

One of the improvements in Storm 0.9.2 is visual depiction of the topology. The following figure is the depiction of a sample topology in the Storm UI:

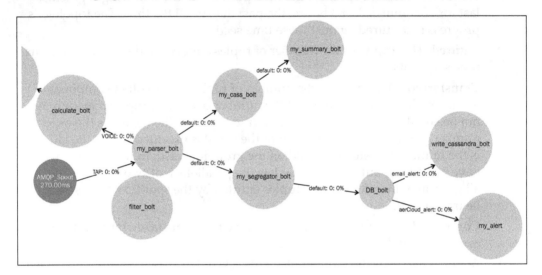

In the preceding screenshot, you can see all the streams visually labeled by various bolts and spouts on the topology along with latency and other key attributes.

The Storm UI provides a very rich interface where the user can start from a very high level and drill down deeper in specific areas, as you can see in the screenshot in *The Storm cluster setup* section where we discussed the Storm cluster level attributes; in the second level, we moved to a specific topology. Next, within a topology, you can click on any bolt or worker and the component level details will be presented to you. One item as highlighted in the following screenshot is of high importance for debugging and log deciphering in cluster setup—the worker ID. If some component spout or bolt is giving us issues and we want to understand the working, the first place to look is the logs. To be able to look at logs, one needs to know where the troublesome bolt is executing which supervisor and which worker; this can be inferred by drilling on that component and looking into the executor section as follows:

The Storm UI capturing the supervisor port

Here, the host tells you which supervisor this component is running on and the port tells you about the worker, so if I want to look for logs of this component, I will look into `logdir` for `sup-flm-dev-1.mydomain.net` in the log directory under `worker-6711.log`.

Storm monitoring tools

The clustered setup of the likes of Storm need constant monitoring, because they are generally developed to support real-time systems wherein downtime could be of concern for **Service Level Agreement** (**SLA**). A lot of tools are available on the market that could be used to monitor the Storm cluster and to raise an alert. Some of the Storm monitoring tools are as follows:

- **Nagios**: This is a very powerful monitoring system that can be extended to generate e-mail alerts. It can monitor various processes and system KPIs and can be tweaked by writing custom scripts and plugins to restart certain components in the event of a failure.

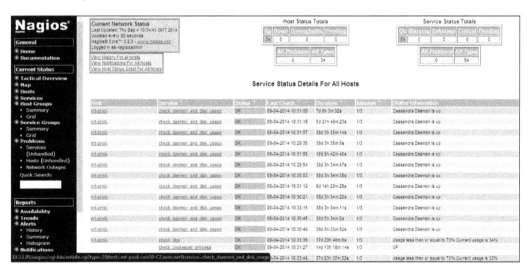

Nagios service console

In the preceding screenshot of a Storm cluster with Nagios monitoring, you can see various processes and other system level KPIs that can be monitored such as CPU, memory, latency, HDD usage, and so on.

- **Ganglia**: This is another widely used open source tool that lets you set up a monitoring framework for Storm clusters.

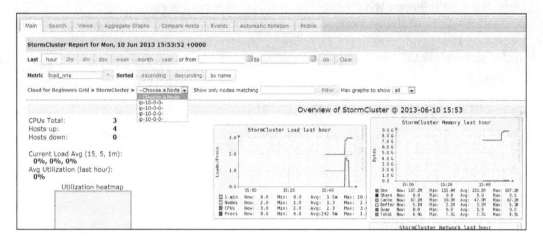

As seen in the preceding screenshot, we have a lot of drill-down options; we can see load and CPU level details as well as other system and cluster level KPIs to capture and plot out the cluster health.

- **SupervisorD**: This is another open source monitoring system that is widely used in conjunction with Storm to capture and retain the health of the cluster. SupervisorD also helps in provisioning and starting the Storm services and it can be configured to restart them in case of any failures.

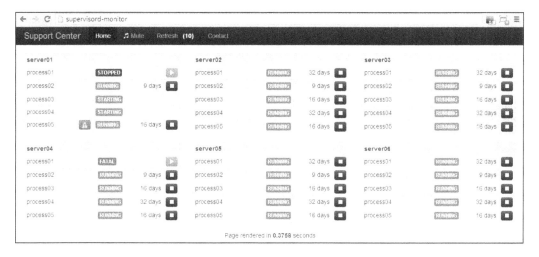

- **Ankush**: This is another provisioning and monitoring system that could be used for Storm and other big data cluster setup and management. It has both paid and open source versions (`https://github.com/impetus-opensource/ankush`). It has the following salient features:

	Environment supported by this application **Physical nodes** **Virtual nodes on Cloud (AWS or On-Premise)**
Provisioning	Single technology clusters
	Multi-technology clusters
	Template-based cluster creation
	Redeploy an erred cluster
	Rack support
	Enhanced node validation before deployment
Monitoring	Heat maps
	Service monitoring
	Technology-based monitoring
	Rich graphs
	Alerts and notifications for key events
	Centralized log view
	Audit trail
	Alerts on dashboard and e-mails

The following screenshot is a dashboard screenshot of Ankush. All the system level KPIs such as CPU, load, network, memory, and so on are very well captured.

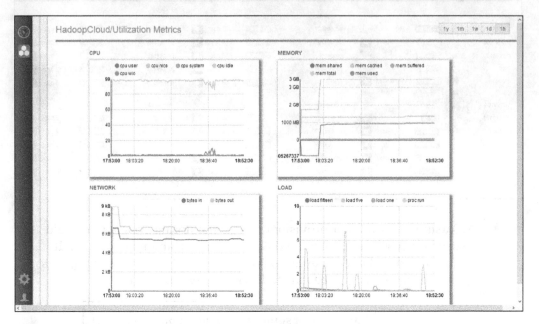

Quiz time

Q.1. State whether the following statements are true or false:

1. The Storm configurations are stored in `cluster.xml`.

2. We can have only four workers allocated per supervisor.

3. The Zookeeper cluster always has an odd number of nodes.

4. Zookeeper needs a minimum of three snapshots to recover its state from failure.

5. A topology can continue to execute if Nimbus and the supervisor dies.

Q.2. Fill in the blanks:

1. _____ is the average time a tuple takes to get processed and acked.

2. _____ is the average time a tuple spends in the execute method.

3. The _____ component is responsible for the recovery of the Storm cluster in the event of a failure.

Q.3. Execute the WordCount topology on a three-node Storm cluster (one Nimbus and two supervisors) and then perform the following tasks:

-   Kill the Nimbus node while the topology is running — observe that the topology will not fail; it will continue unaffected.

-   Kill the supervisor while the topology is running — observe that the topology does not fail, it will continue unaffected. The workers will continue to execute with Zookeeper co-ordination.

-   Try various operations such as rebalance and deactivate from the Storm UI.

Summary

In this chapter, you got a detailed understanding of the Storm and Zookeeper configurations. We explored and walked you through the Storm UI and its attributes. Having done the cluster setup, we briefly touched upon various monitoring tools available for operational production support in Storm.

In the next chapter, we will get you introduced to RabbitMQ and its integration with Storm.

5
Storm High Availability and Failover

This chapter takes you to the next level in your journey through Storm, where we get you acquainted with the integration of Storm with other necessary components in the ecosystem. We will cover the concepts of high availability and reliability, practically.

This chapter is the next step in understanding the clustered mode setup of Storm and its associated components. We will understand the various configurations in Storm and Zookeeper and the concept behind them.

The topics that will be covered in this chapter are as follows:

- Setting up RabbitMQ (single instance and clustered mode)
- Developing the AMQP spout to integrate Storm and RabbitMQ
- Creating a RabbitMQ feeder component
- Building high availability for RabbitMQ and the Storm cluster
- The Storm schedulers

By the end of this chapter, you will be able to set up and understand RabbitMQ and integrate Storm with RabbitMQ. Also, you will be able to test high availability and guaranteed processing of the Storm cluster.

An overview of RabbitMQ

The punch line that goes for RabbitMQ is *Messaging that just works*.

RabbitMQ is one of the most widely used implementations of the AMQP messaging protocol that provides a platform for message receipt and delivery. This in-memory queue also has the capacity to hold and retain messages till they are consumed by a consumer. This flexible brokering system is very easy to use and works on most of the operating systems such as windows, UNIX, and so on.

RabbitMQ is an implementation of the **Advanced Message Queuing Protocol (AMQP)**. As depicted in the following figure, the vital components of RabbitMQ are **exchange** and **Queue**:

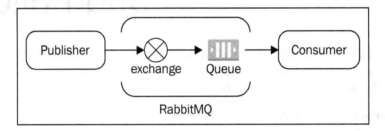

The publisher and the consumer are two essential actors; the former generates the messages and publishes them to the exchange, which in turn (depending upon its type) publishes the message from the publisher to the queue and from the queue to the consumer, who picks up the message.

The point to note is that here the publisher interacts with the exchange and not the queue. There are various kinds of exchanges that RabbitMQ supports such as direct, fanout, topic, and so on. The task of the exchange is to route the message to one or more queues depending upon the type of exchange and the routing key associated with the message. So if it's a direct exchange, the message will be delivered to one queue bound to the exchange with the routing key matching the one in the message. If it's a fanout exchange, then the message is delivered to all the queues bound to the exchange, and the routing is totally ignored.

Installing the RabbitMQ cluster

RabbitMQ is a messaging broker—an intermediary for messaging. It gives your applications a common platform to send and receive messages, and your messages a safe place to live until they are received.

Prerequisites for the setup of RabbitMQ

Make sure you have taken care of the fact that short names are also included in the `/etc/hosts` file as shown in the following code:

```
<ip address1>       <hostname1> <shortname1>
<ip address2>       <hostname2> <shortname2>
```

 Short names in `/etc/hosts` are mandatory because in a RabbitMQ cluster, the internode communication happens using these short names.

For example, we have two machines in our cluster with the following mentioned IPs and hostnames; this information is used by the RabbitMQ daemons while starting the cluster:

```
10.191.206.83       rmq-flc-1.mydomain.net rmq-flc-1
10.73.10.63         rmq-flc-2.mydomain.net rmq-flc-2
```

If the short names are not set, you will see this error: **System NOT running to use fully qualified hostnames**.

Setting up a RabbitMQ server

Ubuntu ships with RabbitMQ but it's often not the latest version. The latest version can be retrieved from RabbitMQ's Debian repository. The following shell script should be run for the RabbitMQ installation on Ubuntu:

```
#!/bin/sh
sudo cat <<EOF > /etc/apt/sources.list.d/rabbitmq.list
sudo deb http://www.rabbitmq.com/debian/ testing main
EOF

sudo curl http://www.rabbitmq.com/rabbitmq-signing-key-public.asc -o
  /tmp/rabbitmq-signing-key-public.asc
sudo apt-key add /tmp/rabbitmq-signing-key-public.asc
sudo rm /tmp/rabbitmq-signing-key-public.asc

sudo apt-get -qy update
sudo apt-get -qy install rabbitmq-server
```

Testing the RabbitMQ server

The following steps will get you the commands that are to be executed on the Ubuntu terminal to start the RabbitMQ server and test it. They are as follows:

1. Start the RabbitMQ server by running the following command on the shell:

```
sudo service rabbitmq-server start
```

```
mp-N155CENTOS6 lib]$ sudo service rabbitmq-server start
Starting rabbitmq-server: SUCCESS
rabbitmq-server.
```

2. Check the server status by running the following command:

```
sudo service rabbitmq-server status
```

```
        N155CENTOS6 lib]$ sudo service rabbitmq-server status
Status of node 'rabbit@   -N155CENTOS6' ...
[{pid,4873},
 {running_applications,[{rabbit,"RabbitMQ","2.8.2"},
                        {os_mon,"CPO   CXC 138 46","2.2.7"},
                        {sasl,"SASL   CXC 138 11","2.1.10"},
                        {mnesia,"MNESIA   CXC 138 12","4.5"},
                        {stdlib,"ERTS   CXC 138 10","1.17.5"},
                        {kernel,"ERTS   CXC 138 10","2.14.5"}]},
 {os,{unix,linux}},
 {erlang_version,"Erlang R14B04 (erts-5.8.5) [source] [smp:4:4] [rq:4] [async-th
reads:30] [kernel-poll:true]\n"},
 {memory,[{total,13428408},
         {processes,5109876},
         {processes_used,5101804},
         {system,8318532},
         {atom,749857},
         {atom_used,748227},
         {binary,82000},
         {code,5991828},
         {ets,391640}]},
 {vm_memory_high_watermark,0.3999999999001241},
 {vm_memory_limit,1601988198},
 {disk_free_limit,4004970496},
 {disk_free,350537601024},
 {file_descriptors,[{total_limit,924},
                    {total_used,3},
                    {sockets_limit,829},
                    {sockets_used,1}]},
 {processes,[{limit,1048576},{used,121}]},
 {run_queue,0},
 {uptime,88}]
...done.
```

3. On each RabbitMQ instance, to enable the RabbitMQ management console, execute the following command and restart the RabbitMQ server running on that instance, by using the following command:

```
sudo rabbitmq-plugins enable rabbitmq_management
```

4. To enable the RabbitMQ plugins, navigate to `/usr/lib/rabbitmq/bin` and execute the following command on both nodes and restart them:

```
sudo rabbitmq-plugins enable rabbitmq_management
```

5. Startup, shutdown, and error logs are created under the `/var/log/rabbitmq` directory.

Creating a RabbitMQ cluster

Here are the steps that you need to execute to set up a two (or more) node RabbitMQ cluster:

1. Considering `rmq-flc-1` and `rmq-flc-2` are the short hostnames of the two instances, we will start standalone RabbitMQ servers on both instances using the command:

```
sudo service rabbitmq-server start
```

2. On `rmq-flc-2`, we will stop the RabbitMQ application, reset the node, join the cluster, and restart the RabbitMQ application using the following commands (all this is being done while the RabbitMQ server is up and running on `rmq-flc-1`):

```
sudo rabbitmqctl stop_app
sudo rabbitmqctl join_cluster rabbit@rmq-flc-1
sudo rabbitmqctl start_app
```

3. Check the cluster status by running the following command on any of the machines:

```
sudo service rabbitmq-server status
```

4. The following output should be seen:

```
[         -N155CENTOS6 lib]$ cat /var/lib/rabbitmq/.er^C
[         -N155CENTOS6 lib]$ su -
Password:
[root@   -N155CENTOS6 ~]# cat /var/lib/rabbitmq/.erlang.cookie
CEHGLTMXKCHVXBIOFYVY
(reverse-i-search)`echo': ^Cho CEHGLTMXKCHVXBIOFYVY > /var/lib/rabbitmq/.erlang.coo
kie
[root@   -N155CENTOS6 ~]# exit
logout
[         -N155CENTOS6 lib]$ sudo rabbitmqctl cluster_status
[sudo] password:
Cluster status of node 'rabbit@   -N155CENTOS6' ...
[{nodes,[{disc,[rabbit@goofy,'rabbit@   -N155CENTOS6']}]},
 {running_nodes,[rabbit@goofy,'rabbit@   -N155CENTOS6']}]
...done.
```

5. The cluster is set up successfully.

The cluster can be accessed at `http://<hostip>:15672` (username: `guest`, password: `guest`), if the UI is enabled.

Enabling the RabbitMQ UI

Perform the following steps to enable the RabbitMQ UI:

1. Execute the following command:

   ```
   sudo /usr/lib/rabbitmq/bin/rabbitmq-plugins enable
       rabbitmq_management
   ```

2. The preceding command will result in the following output:

   ```
   The following plugins have been enabled:
   mochiweb

   webmachine
   rabbitmq_mochiweb
   amqp_client
   rabbitmq_management_agent
   rabbitmq_management
   Plugin configuration has changed. Restart RabbitMQ for changes to
   take effect.
   ```

3. Repeat the preceding steps on all nodes of the cluster.

4. Restart each node using the following command:

   ```
   sudo service rabbitmq-server restart
   ```

5. Access the UI using the `http://<hostip>:15672` link. The default username and password is `guest`.

Creating mirror queues for high availability

In this section, we talk about a special kind of queues that guarantee high availability over the RabbitMQ default queues. By default, the queues that we create are located on a single node based on the order in which they are declared, and this can become the single point of failure. Let's look at an example. I have a cluster of two RabbitMQ nodes, `rabbit1` and `rabbit2`, and I declare one exchange over my cluster, say, `myrabbitxchange`. Let's say by the order of execution, the queue is created in `rabbit1`. Now if `rabbit1` goes down, then the queue is gone and the clients will not be able to publish to it.

Thus to avoid situations, we need highly available queues; they are called mirrored queues, which are replicated on all the nodes in the cluster. Mirrored queues have one master and multiple slaves, the oldest one is the master and if it's not available, the oldest amongst the available nodes becomes the master. Messages are published to all slaves. This enhances the availability but doesn't distribute the load. To create the mirror queues, use the following steps:

1. Mirroring can be enabled by adding a policy using the web UI. Go to the **Admin** tab and select **Policies** and click on **Add policy**.

2. Specify policy **Name**, **Pattern**, **Definition**, and click on **Add Policy**, as shown in the following screenshot:

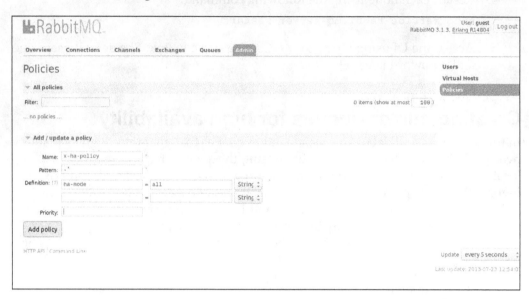

Integrating Storm with RabbitMQ

Now that we have installed Storm, the next step will be to integrate RabbitMQ with Storm, for which we will have to create a custom spout called the RabbitMQ spout. This spout will read the messages from the specified queue; thus, it will furnish the role of a consumer, and then push these messages to a downstream topology.

Here is how the spout code will look:

```
public class AMQPRecvSpout implements IRichSpout{

//The constructor where we set initialize all properties
  public AMQPRecvSpout(String host, int port, String username,
  String password, String vhost, boolean requeueOnFail, boolean
  autoAck) {
    this.amqpHost = host;
    this.amqpPort = port;
    this.amqpUsername = username;
    this.amqpPasswd = password;
    this.amqpVhost = vhost;
    this.requeueOnFail = requeueOnFail;
    this.autoAck = autoAck;
  }
```

```
/*
Open method of the spout , here we initialize the prefetch count ,
  this parameter specified how many messages would be prefetched
  from the queue by the spout - to increase the efficiency of the
  solution */
  public void open(@SuppressWarnings("rawtypes") Map conf,
  TopologyContext context, SpoutOutputCollector collector) {
    Long prefetchCount = (Long) conf.get(CONFIG_PREFETCH_COUNT);
    if (prefetchCount == null) {
      log.info("Using default prefetch-count");
      prefetchCount = DEFAULT_PREFETCH_COUNT;
    } else if (prefetchCount < 1) {
      throw new IllegalArgumentException(CONFIG_PREFETCH_COUNT + "
      must be at least 1");
    }
    this.prefetchCount = prefetchCount.intValue();

    try {
      this.collector = collector;
      setupAMQP();
    } catch (IOException e) {
      log.error("AMQP setup failed", e);
      log.warn("AMQP setup failed, will attempt to reconnect...");
      Utils.sleep(WAIT_AFTER_SHUTDOWN_SIGNAL);
      reconnect();
    }
  }


  /**
   * Reconnect to an AMQP broker.in case the connection breaks at
   some point
   */
  private void reconnect() {
    log.info("Reconnecting to AMQP broker...");
    try {
      setupAMQP();
    } catch (IOException e) {
      log.warn("Failed to reconnect to AMQP broker", e);
    }
  }
  /**
   * Set up a connection with an AMQP broker.
   * @throws IOException
   *This is the method where we actually connect to the queue
   using AMQP client APIs
```

```
    */
    private void setupAMQP() throws IOException{
      final int prefetchCount = this.prefetchCount;
      final ConnectionFactory connectionFactory = new
      ConnectionFactory() {
        public void configureSocket(Socket socket)
            throws IOException {
          socket.setTcpNoDelay(false);
          socket.setReceiveBufferSize(20*1024);
          socket.setSendBufferSize(20*1024);
        }
      };

      connectionFactory.setHost(amqpHost);
      connectionFactory.setPort(amqpPort);
      connectionFactory.setUsername(amqpUsername);
      connectionFactory.setPassword(amqpPasswd);
      connectionFactory.setVirtualHost(amqpVhost);

      this.amqpConnection = connectionFactory.newConnection();
      this.amqpChannel = amqpConnection.createChannel();
      log.info("Setting basic.qos prefetch-count to " +
      prefetchCount);
      amqpChannel.basicQos(prefetchCount);
      amqpChannel.exchangeDeclare(Constants.EXCHANGE_NAME,
      "direct");
      amqpChannel.queueDeclare(Constants.QUEUE_NAME, true, false,
      false, null);
      amqpChannel.queueBind(Constants.QUEUE_NAME,
      Constants.EXCHANGE_NAME, "");
      this.amqpConsumer = new QueueingConsumer(amqpChannel);
      assert this.amqpConsumer != null;
      this.amqpConsumerTag =
      amqpChannel.basicConsume(Constants.QUEUE_NAME, this.autoAck,
      amqpConsumer);
    }

    /*
     * Cancels the queue subscription, and disconnects from the AMQP
     broker.
     */
    public void close() {
      try {
        if (amqpChannel != null) {
          if (amqpConsumerTag != null) {
```

```
        amqpChannel.basicCancel(amqpConsumerTag);
      }
      amqpChannel.close();
    }
  } catch (IOException e) {
    log.warn("Error closing AMQP channel", e);
  }

  try {
    if (amqpConnection != null) {
      amqpConnection.close();
    }
  } catch (IOException e) {
    log.warn("Error closing AMQP connection", e);
  }
}
/*
 * Emit message received from queue into collector
 */
public void nextTuple() {
  if (spoutActive && amqpConsumer != null) {
    try {
      final QueueingConsumer.Delivery delivery =
      amqpConsumer.nextDelivery(WAIT_FOR_NEXT_MESSAGE);
      if (delivery == null) return;
      final long deliveryTag =
      delivery.getEnvelope().getDeliveryTag();
      String message = new String(delivery.getBody());

      if (message != null && message.length() > 0) {
        collector.emit(new Values(message), deliveryTag);
      } else {
        log.debug("Malformed deserialized message, null or zero-
        length. " + deliveryTag);
        if (!this.autoAck) {
          ack(deliveryTag);
        }
      }
    } catch (ShutdownSignalException e) {
      log.warn("AMQP connection dropped, will attempt to
      reconnect...");
      Utils.sleep(WAIT_AFTER_SHUTDOWN_SIGNAL);
      reconnect();
    } catch (ConsumerCancelledException e) {
```

```
        log.warn("AMQP consumer cancelled, will attempt to
        reconnect...");
        Utils.sleep(WAIT_AFTER_SHUTDOWN_SIGNAL);
        reconnect();
      } catch (InterruptedException e) {
        log.error("Interrupted while reading a message, with
        Exception : " +e);
      }
    }
  }
  /*
   * ack method to acknowledge the message that is successfully
   processed
 */

  public void ack(Object msgId) {
    if (msgId instanceof Long) {
      final long deliveryTag = (Long) msgId;
      if (amqpChannel != null) {
        try {
          amqpChannel.basicAck(deliveryTag, false);
        } catch (IOException e) {
          log.warn("Failed to ack delivery-tag " + deliveryTag,
          e);
        } catch (ShutdownSignalException e) {
          log.warn("AMQP connection failed. Failed to ack
          delivery-tag " + deliveryTag, e);
        }
      }
    } else {
      log.warn(String.format("don't know how to ack(%s: %s)",
      msgId.getClass().getName(), msgId));
    }
  }

  public void fail(Object msgId) {
    if (msgId instanceof Long) {
      final long deliveryTag = (Long) msgId;
      if (amqpChannel != null) {
        try {
          if (amqpChannel.isOpen()) {
            if (!this.autoAck) {
              amqpChannel.basicReject(deliveryTag, requeueOnFail);
            }
```

```
                } else {
                  reconnect();
                }
            } catch (IOException e) {
                log.warn("Failed to reject delivery-tag " + deliveryTag,
                e);
            }
          }
        } else {
          log.warn(String.format("don't know how to reject(%s: %s)",
          msgId.getClass().getName(), msgId));
        }
    }
  }

  public void declareOutputFields(OutputFieldsDeclarer declarer) {
      declarer.declare(new Fields("messages"));
  }
}
```

AMQP Maven dependency that will be required to be introduced in the project
`pom.xml`, as shown in the following code:

```
<dependency>
  <groupId>com.rabbitmq</groupId>
  <artifactId>amqp-client</artifactId>
  <version>3.2.1</version>
</dependency>
```

Creating a RabbitMQ feeder component

Now that we have installed the RabbitMQ cluster, all we need is to develop a
publisher component that will publish the messages to RabbitMQ. This will be
a simple Java component that will mimic the live feed to RabbitMQ. The basic
code snippet for this is as follows:

```
public class FixedEmitter {
  private static final String EXCHANGE_NAME = "MYExchange";
  public static void main(String[] argv) throws Exception {
    /*we are creating a new connection factory for builing
    connections with exchange*/
    ConnectionFactory factory = new ConnectionFactory();
    /* we are specifying the RabbitMQ host address and port here
    in */
```

```java
Address[] addressArr = {
  new Address("localhost", 5672)
}; //specify the IP if the queue is not on local node where
this program would execute
Connection connection = factory.newConnection(addressArr);
//creating a channel for rabbitMQ
Channel channel = connection.createChannel();
//Declaring the queue and routing key
String queueName = "MYQueue";
String routingKey = "MYQueue";
//Declaring the Exchange
channel.exchangeDeclare(EXCHANGE_NAME, "direct", false);
Map < String, Object > args = new HashMap < String, Object >
();
//defining the queue policy
args.put("x-ha-policy", "all");
//declaring and binding the queue to the exchange
channel.queueDeclare(queueName, true, false, false, args);
channel.queueBind(queueName, EXCHANGE_NAME, routingKey);
String stoppedRecord;
int i = 0;
//emitting sample records
while (i < 1) {
  try {
    myRecord = "MY Sample record";
    channel.basicPublish(EXCHANGE_NAME, routingKey,
      MessageProperties.PERSISTENT_TEXT_PLAIN,
      myRecord.getBytes());
    System.out.println(" [x] Sent '" + myRecord + "' sent at "
    + new Date());
    i++;
    Thread.sleep(2);
  } catch (Exception e) {
    e.printStackTrace();
  }
}
channel.close();
connection.close();
  }
}
```

Wiring the topology for the AMQP spout

Now we have the clustered queue setup ready, the AMQP spout in place, and the feeder component in place; let's put the last and final piece in place, that's the overall integration of the Storm topology.

Let's use our `WordCount` topology again and instead of `RandomSentenceSpout` we will use `AMQPRecvSpout`, which we designed in the previous section, *Integrating Storm with RabbitMQ*.

The following code chunk needs to be modified:

```
builder.setSpout("spout", new RandomSentenceSpout(), 5);
builder.setBolt("split", new SplitSentence(),
  8).shuffleGrouping("spout");
We will use the new spout instead, as follows:


builder.setSpout("queue_reader", new
  AMQPRecvSpout(Constants.RMQ_ADDRESS, 5672, "guest", "guest",
  "/"));
```

Building high availability of components

Now we are at an opportune juncture to look for high availability of various components in the cluster. We will do this as a series of exercises wherein we assume that each component is installed in the clustered mode and more than one instance of it exists in the ecosystem.

The high availability of RabbitMQ can be checked only after you have a mirrored queue in place. Let's assume:

- We have two nodes in the RabbitMQ cluster: node1 and node2
- `MyExchange` is the name of the exchange that is created for the purpose of this exercise
- `MyQueue` is a mirrored queue that is created for this exercise

Next, we will just run the `fixedEmitter` code we created in the *Creating a RabbitMQ feeder component* section. Now perform the Litmus test:

- Let's assume the queue `MyQueue` has 100 messages
- Now bring down node2 (this means, one node on the cluster is down)
- All the 100 messages will be retained and will be visible on the console; node1 fills in when there is an absence of node2

This behavior ensures that services are not disrupted even if a node in the cluster goes down.

High availability of the Storm cluster

Now let's see the demonstration of a failover or high availability in Storm. The Storm framework is built in such a way that it can continue to execute as long as:

- It has the required number of Zookeeper connections
- It has the required number of workers on one or more supervisors

So what do the preceding statements actually mean? Well, let's understand this with an example. Let's say I am executing the WordCount topology on a Storm cluster. This cluster has the following configuration:

- There are two Storm supervisors with four workers on each Storm supervisor, so a total eight workers in the cluster
- There are three Zookeeper nodes (max connections 30), so in total 30*2*3=180 connections
- A topology is allocated with three workers

Let's assume when we submit this topology onto the cluster, the tasks and processes are spawned as shown in the following screenshot:

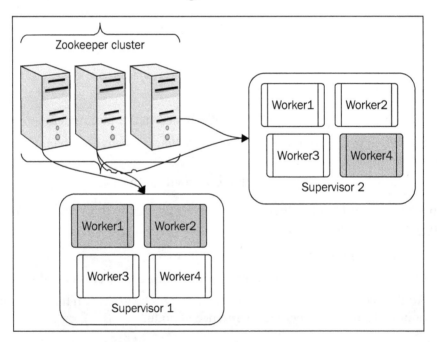

The preceding figure depicts the cluster diagrammatically and the gray workers are the ones that are allocated to the topology. Now we are all set to try out the high availability test for Storm and Zookeeper. The tests for Storm and Zookeeper are as follows:

- **Test 1** (all components are up and the topology is running): Kill the Nimbus node after the topology is submitted; you will notice that the topology will continue to execute normally.

- **Test 2** (all components are up and the topology is running): Kill one Zookeeper node and you will notice that the topology will continue to execute normally, because two of the other available Zookeepers have sufficient resources in terms of connections that can keep the Storm cluster up and running.

- **Test 3** (all components are up and the topology is running): Kill two Zookeeper nodes and you will notice that the topology will continue to execute normally, because one of the other two available Zookeepers have sufficient resources in terms of connections that they can keep the Storm cluster up and running.

- **Test 4** (all components are up and the topology is running): Kill supervisor 2; now we have one of the gray workers on this node. So when this node goes down, the gray worker dies, and then because the second supervisor is not available it's spawned again, this time on supervisor 1. So all workers of the topology will be executing on one single supervisor now, but the system will continue to perform with limited resources but will not fail.

Guaranteed processing of the Storm cluster

The next topic to discuss in this section is to see *Storm's guaranteed message processing in action*. We discussed this concept in previous chapters, but to understand it practically, I didn't go into depth because I wanted to introduce you all to the AMQP spout first. Now let's go back to the example we discussed in *Chapter 2, Getting Started with Your First Topology*.

Now as depicted in the following figure, the dash arrow flow shows that the events that fail to process are re-queued to the queue:

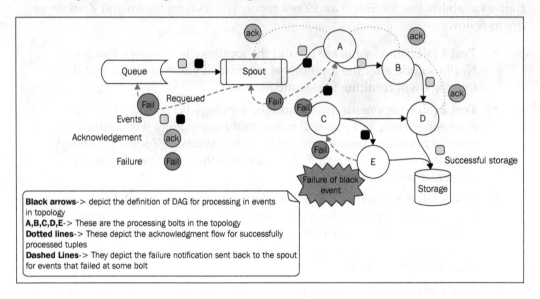

Now let's tweak our `wordCount` topology a bit where we had added `AMQPRecvSpout` to fail the events, and see where they actually show up. Let's assume I used `FixedEmitter` to emit 10 events into the queue. Now I tweak my `wordCount` bolt and induce artificial sleep for five minutes in the execute method, so that every event is held there for 300 seconds (using `Thread.sleep(300)`). This will lead to its timeout as the default event timeout is 60 seconds.

Now when you run the topology, you will be able to see the events being re-queued back to RabbitMQ using the UI.

The Storm isolation scheduler

The Storm isolation scheduler was released in Storm Version 0.8.2. This was a very handy feature that is very actively being used ever since its release, in the case of the shared Storm cluster. Let's understand its working and capability through an example; say, we have a four supervisor node Storm cluster with four slots each, so in total I have 16 slots. Now I want to employ three Storm topologies here, say, Topo1, Topo2, and Topo3; each has four workers allocated to it.

So by probable default, the scheduling behavior of the Storm distribution will be as follows:

	Supervisor 1	Supervisor 2	Supervisor 3	Supervisor 4
Topo1	Worker 1	Worker 2	Worker 3	Worker 4
Topo2	Worker 2	Worker 1	Worker 1	Worker 1
Topo3	Worker 3	Worker 3	Worker 2	Worker 2

Storm will respect load distribution and will spawn one worker of each topology on each node.

Now let's tweak the scenario a bit and introduce a requirement that Topo1 is a very resource-intensive topology. (I want to dedicate one supervisor entirely to this one so that I save on network hops.) This could be attained by the use of the isolation scheduler.

We will have to make the following entry in the `storm.yaml` file of each Storm node in the cluster (Nimbus and supervisor):

```
isolation.scheduler.machines:
    "Topo1": 2
```

The cluster is required to be restarted for this setting to take effect. This setting means that we have dedicated two supervisor nodes to Topo1 and it will be no longer be shared with other topologies being submitted to the cluster. This will also ensure a viable solution to multitenancy problems encountered in production.

The other two supervisors will be shared amongst Topo2 and Topo3. The probable distribution will be as follows:

	Supervisor 1	Supervisor 2	Supervisor 3	Supervisor 4
Topo1	Worker 1 Worker 2	Worker 1 Worker 2		
Topo2			Worker 1 Worker 2	Worker 1 Worker 2
Topo3			Worker 3 Worker 4	Worker 3 Worker 4

So, as evident from the preceding table, Topo1 will be isolated to Supervisor1 and 2 while Top2 and Topo3 will share the remaining eight slots on the Supervisor3 and 4.

Quiz time

Q.1 State whether the following sentences are true or false:

1. AMQP is a STOMP protocol.
2. RabbitMQ is not fail-safe.
3. An AMQP client is required to publish to RabbitMQ.
4. A mirrored queue can recover from the failure of nodes in a cluster.

Q.2 Fill in the blanks:

1. _____ is the exchange where messages are delivered based on the routing key.
2. _____ is the exchange where messages are broadcasted.
3. The _____ is an implementation of the Storm spout on the AMQP consumer protocol.

Q.3 Execute the WordCount topology on a three node Storm cluster (one nimbus and two supervisor nodes) clubbed with a two node RabbitMQ cluster:

- Try out various failure scenarios mentioned in the *Building high availability of components* section
- Induce an artificial delay in message processing to calibrate the guaranteed processing of the Storm topology

Summary

In this chapter, you have understood the RabbitMQ implementation of the AMQP protocol. We completed the cluster setup and integrated the output of the Storm topology with the queues. We also explored and practically tested the scenarios of high availability and reliability for both RabbitMQ and Storm. We closed the chapter by touching upon the Storm schedulers. In the next chapter, we will get acquainted with Storm persistence using Cassandra.

6
Adding NoSQL Persistence to Storm

In this chapter, we will graduate to the next step in understanding Storm—we will add persistence to our topology. We have chosen Cassandra for very obvious reasons, which will be elaborated during this chapter. The intent is to make you understand how the Cassandra data store can be integrated with the Storm topology.

The following topics will be covered in this chapter:

- The advantages of Cassandra
- Introduction to columnar databases and column family design fundamentals
- Setting up a Cassandra cluster
- Introducing the CQLSH, CLI, and Connector APIs
- Storm topology wired to the Cassandra store
- Understanding the mechanism of persistence
- The best practices for Storm Cassandra applications

The advantages of Cassandra

This is the first and most obvious question anyone would ask, "Why are we using NoSQL?" Well, the very quick answer for looking at NoSQL instead of traditional data stores is the same as why the world is moving to big data—low cost, highly scalable, and reliable solutions that can store endless amounts of data.

Now, the next question is why Cassandra, and why not anything else out of the NoSQL stack. Here the answer lies in the kind of problem and solution approach we are trying to implement. Well, we are handling real-time analytics, and everything we need should be accurate, fail-safe, and lightning fast. Therefore, Cassandra is the best choice because:

- It has the fastest writes amongst its peers such as HBase and so on
- It is linearly scalable with peer-to-peer design
- No single point of failure
- Read and write requests can be handled without impacting each other's performance
- Handles search queries comprising millions of transactions and lightning-fast speeds
- Fail-safe and highly available with replication factors in place
- Guarantees eventual consistency with the CAP theorem on NoSQL DBs
- Column family design to handle a variety of formats
- No or low licensing cost
- Less development-ops or operational cost
- It can be extended for integration on a variety of other big data components

Columnar database fundamentals

One of the most important aspects of getting started with NoSQL data stores is getting to understand the fundamentals of columnar databases; or rather, let's use the actual term—column families.

This is a concept that has a variety of implementations in different NoSQL databases, for instance:

- **Cassandra**: This is a key-value-pair-based NoSQL DB
- **Mongo DB**: This is a document-based NoSQL DB
- **Neo4J**: This is a graph DB

They differ from conventional RDBMS systems that are row-oriented in terms of the following:

- Performance
- Storage extendibility
- Fault tolerance
- Low or no licensing cost

But having iterated all the differences and benefits of NoSQL DBs, you must clearly understand that the shift to NoSQL is a shift of the entire paradigm of data storage, availability, and access — they are not a replacement for RDBMS.

In the RDBMS world, we are all used to creating tables, but here in Cassandra, we create column families where we define the metadata of the columns, but the columns are actually stored as rows. Each row can have different sets of columns, thus making the whole column family relatively unstructured and extendible.

Types of column families

There are two types of column families:

- **Static column family**: As the name suggests, this has a static set of columns and is a very close surrogate of all well-known RDBMS tables, barring a few differences that are a result of its NoSQL heritage. Here is an example of a static column family:

Rowkey	Columns			
Raman	Name	E-mail	Cell no.	Age
	Raman Subramanian	aa@yahoo.com	9999999999	20
Edison	Name	E-mail	Cell no.	Age
	Edison Weasley	bb@yahoo.com	88888888888	30
Amey	Name	E-mail	Cell no.	Age
	Amey Marriot	cc@yahoo.com	7777777777	40
Sriman	Name	E-mail		
	Sriman Mishra	dd@yahoo.com		

- **Dynamic column family**: This one gets the true essence of being unstructured and schema-less. Here, we don't use predefined columns associated with the column family, but the same can be dynamically generated and supplied by the client application at the time of inserting data into the column family. During the creation or definition of a dynamic column family, we get to define the information about the column names and values by defining the comparators and validators. Here is an example of a dynamic column family:

Rowkey	Columns			
Raman	Name	E-mail	Cell no.	Age
Edison	Address	State	Territory	
Amey	Country	Sex	Cell no.	Age
Sriman	Nationality			

Types of columns

There are a variety of columns that Cassandra supports:

- **Standard columns**: These columns contain a name; this is either static or dynamic and set by the writing application. A value (this is actually the attribute that stores the data) and timestamp are shown here:

Column_name
value
timestamp

  Cassandra makes use of the timestamp associated with the column to find out the last update to the column. When data is queried from Cassandra, it orders by this timestamp and always returns the most recent value.

- **Composite columns**: Cassandra makes use of this storage mechanism to handle clustered rows. This is a unique way of handling all the logical rows together that share the same partition key into a single physical wide row. This enables Cassandra to accomplish the legendary feat of storing 2 billion columns per row. For example, let's say I want to create a table where I capture live status updates from some social networking sites:

```
CREATE TABLE statusUpdates(
    update_id uuid PRIMARY KEY,
    username varchar,
    mesage varchar
    );

CREATE TABLE timeseriesTable (
    user_id varchar,
```

```
  udate_id uuid,
  username varchar,
  mesage varchar,
  PRIMARY KEY user_id , update_id )
);
```

The live updates are being recorded under the `StatusUpdates` table that has the `username`, `message`, and `update_id` (which is actually a UUID) property.

While designing a Cassandra column family, you should make extensive use of the functionality provided by UUIDs, which can be employed for sequencing data.

The combination of the `user_id` and `update_id` properties from `timeseriesTable` can uniquely identify a row in chronology.

Cassandra makes use of the first column defined in the primary key as the partition key; this is also known as the row key.

- **Expiring columns**: These are special types of Cassandra columns that have a time to live (**TTL**) associated with them; the values stored in these columns are automatically deleted or erased after the TTL has elapsed. These columns are used for use cases where we don't want to retain data older than a stated interval; for instance, if we don't need data older than 24 hours. In our column family, I would associate a TTL of 24 hours with every column that is being inserted, and this data will be automatically deleted by Cassandra after 24 hours of its insertion.

- **Counter columns**: These are again specialized function columns that store a number incrementally. They have a special implementation and a specialized usage for situations where we use counters; for instance, if I need to count the number of occurrences of an event.

Setting up the Cassandra cluster

Cassandra is a very scalable key-value store. It promises eventual consistency and its distributed ring-based architecture eliminates any single point of failure in the cluster, thus making it highly available. It's designed and developed to support very fast reads and writes over excessively large volumes of data .This fast write and read ability makes it a very strong contender to be used in an **online transaction processing** (OLTP) application to support large business intelligence systems.

Cassandra provides a column-family-based data model that is more flexible than typical key-value systems.

Installing Cassandra

Cassandra requires the most stable version of Java 1.6 that you can deploy, preferably the Oracle or Sun JVM. Perform the following steps to install Cassandra:

1. Download the most recent stable release (version 1.1.6 at the time of writing) from the Apache Cassandra site.

2. Create a Cassandra directory under `/usr/local` as follows:

   ```
   sudo mkdir /usr/local/cassandra
   ```

3. Extract the downloaded TAR file to the `/usr/local` location. Use the following command:

   ```
   sudo tar -xvf apache-cassandra-1.1.6-bin.tar.gz -C
   /usr/local/cassandra
   ```

4. Cassandra needs a directory to store its data, log files, and cache files. Create `/usr/local/cassandra/tmp` to store this data:

   ```
   sudo mkdir -p /usr/local/cassandra/tmp
   ```

5. Update the `Cassandra.yaml` configuration file under `/usr/local/Cassandra/apache-cassandra-1.1.6/conf`.

   The following properties will go into it:

   ```
   cluster_name: 'MyClusterName'
   seeds: <IP of Node-1><IP of Node-2>(IP address of each node
     go into it)
   listen_address: <IP of Current Node>
   ```

6. Calculate a token for each node using the following script and update the `initial_token` property to each node by adding a unique token value in `Cassandra.yaml`:

   ```
   #! /usr/bin/python
   import sys
   if (len(sys.argv) > 1):
     num=int(sys.argv[1])
   else:
     num=int(raw_input("How many nodes are in your cluster?
     "))
   for i in range(0, num):
     print 'node %d: %d' % (i, (i*(2**127)/num))
   ```

7. Update the following property in the `conf/log4j-server.properties` file. Create the `temp` directory under `cassandra`:

   `Log4j.appender.R.File=/usr/local/cassandra/temp/system.log`

8. Increase the `rpc_timeout` property in `Cassandra.yaml` (if this timeout is very small and the network latency is high, Cassandra might assume the nodes are dead without waiting long enough for a response to propagate).

9. Run the Cassandra server at `/usr/local/Cassandra/apache-cassandra-1.1.6` using `bin/Cassandra -f`.

10. Run the Cassandra client at `/usr/local/Cassandra/apache-cassandra-1.1.6` using `bin/Cassandra-cli` with a host and port.

11. Use the `bin/nodetool` ring utility at `/usr/local/Cassandra/apache-cassandra-1.1.6` to verify a properly connected cluster:

```
bin/nodetool –host <ip-adress> -p <port number> ring
192.168.1.30 datacenter1 rack1 Up     Normal 755.25 MB
   25.00% 0
192.168.1.31 datacenter1 rack1 Up     Normal 400.62 MB
   25.00% 42535295865117307932921825928970
192.168.1.51 datacenter1 rack1 Up     Normal 400.62 MB
   25.00% 42535295865117307932921825928971
192.168.1.32 datacenter1 rack1 Up     Normal 793.06 MB
   25.00% 85070591730234615865843651857941
```

The preceding output displays a connected cluster. This configuration shows that it's correctly configured and connected.

Here is a screenshot of the output:

```
bin/nodetool -host 10.176.0.146 ring
Address         Status    Load      Range                                           Ring
10.176.0.146    Up        459.27 MB 75603446264197340449435394672681112420          |<--|
10.176.1.161    Up        382.53 MB 137462771597874153173150284137310597304         |   |
10.176.1.162    Up        511.34 MB 63538518574533451921556363897953848387          |-->|
```

Multiple data centers

In practical scenarios, we would want to have Cassandra clusters distributed across different data centers so that the system is more reliable and resilient overall to localized network snags and physical disasters.

Prerequisites for setting up multiple data centers

The following are a set of prerequisites that should be used for setting up multiple data centers:

- Have Cassandra installed on each node
- Have the IP address of each node in the cluster
- Identify the cluster names
- Identify the seed nodes
- Identify the snitch that is to be used

Installing Cassandra data centers

The following are a set of steps to set up Cassandra data centers:

1. Let's start with an assumption that we have already installed Cassandra on the following nodes:

   10.188.66.41 (seed1)

   10.196.43.66

   10.188.247.41

   10.196.170.59 (seed2)

   10.189.61.170

   10.189.30.138

2. Assign tokens using the token generation Python script defined in the previous section to each of the preceding nodes.

3. Let's say we align to the following distribution of nodes and their tokens across the data centers:

Node	IP Address	Token	Data Center
node0	10.188.66.41	0	Dc1
node1	10.196.43.66	56713727820156410577229101238628035245	Dc1
node2	10.188.247.41	113427455564031282115445820247725607 0488	Dc1
node3	10.196.170.59	10	Dc2
node4	10.189.61.170	56713727820156410577229101238628035255	Dc2
node5	10.189.30.138	113427455564031282115445820247725607 0498	Dc2

4. Stop Cassandra on the nodes and clear the data from `data_dir` of Cassandra:

    ```
    $ ps auwx | grep cassandra
    ```

    This command finds the Cassandra Java process ID (PID):

    ```
    $ sudo kill <pid>
    ```

    This is the command to kill the process with the specified PID:

    ```
    $ sudo rm -rf /var/lib/cassandra/*
    ```

    The preceding command clears the data from the default directories of Cassandra.

5. Modify the following property settings in the `cassandra.yaml` file for each node:

    ```
    endpoint_snitch <provide the name of snitch>
      initial_token: <provide the value of token from previous
      step>
      seeds: <provide internal IP_address of each seed node>
      listen_address: <provide localhost IP address>
    ```

    Here is what the updated configuration will look like:

    ```
    node0:
    end_point_snitch:
      org.apache.cassandra.locator.PropertyFileSnitch
    initial_token: 0
    seed_provider:
      - class_name:
      org.apache.cassandra.locator.SimpleSeedProvider
      parameters:
      - seeds: "10.188.66.41,10.196.170.59"
      listen_address: 10.196.43.66
      node1 to node5
    ```

    All the properties for these nodes are the same as those defined for the preceding `node0` except for the `initial_token` and `listen_address` properties.

6. Next, we will have to assign names to each data center and their racks; for example, `Dc1`, `Dc2` and `Rc1`, `Rc2`.

7. Go to the `cassandra-topology.properties` file and add an assignment for data center and rack names against the IP addresses of each node. For example:

    ```
    # Cassandra Node IP=Data Center:Rack
    10.188.66.41=Dc1:Rc1
    10.196.43.66=Dc2:Rc1
    10.188.247.41=Dc1:Rc1
    10.196.170.59=Dc2:Rc1
    10.189.61.170=Dc1:Rc1
    10.199.30.138=Dc2:Rc1
    ```

8. The next step is to start seed nodes one by one, followed by all the rest of the nodes.

9. Check that your ring is up and running.

Introduction to CQLSH

Now that we are through with the Cassandra setup, let's get acquainted with the shell and a few basic commands:

1. Run CQL at `/usr/local/Cassandra/apache-cassandra-1.1.6` using `bin/cqlsh` with a host and port:

    ```
    bin/cqlsh  -host <ip-adress> -p <port number>
    ```

2. Create a keyspace either at the Cassandra client or at CQL, as follows:

    ```
    create keyspace <keyspace_name>;
    ```

3. Create a column family at the Cassandra client or at CQL as follows:

    ```
    use <keyspace_name>;
    create column family <columnfamily name>;
    ```

    For example, create the following table:

    ```
    CREATE TABLE appUSers (
      user_name varchar,
      Dept varchar,
      email varchar,
      PRIMARY KEY (user_name));
    ```

4. Insert a few records into the column family from the command line:

    ```
    INSERT INTO appUSers (user_name, Dept, email)
      VALUES ('shilpi', 'bigdata, 'shilpisaxena@yahoo.com');
    ```

5. Retrieve the data from the column family:

```
SELECT * FROM appUSers LIMIT 10;
```

Introduction to CLI

This section gets you acquainted with another tool that is used for interaction with Cassandra processes—the CLI shell.

The following steps are used for interacting with Cassandra using the CLI shell:

1. The following is the command to connect to the Cassandra CLI:

```
Cd Cassandra-installation-dir/bin
cassandra-cli -host localhost -port 9160
```

2. Create a keyspace:

```
[default@unknown] CREATE KEYSPACE myKeySpace
with placement_strategy = 'SimpleStrategy'
and strategy_options = {replication_factor:1};
```

3. Verify the creation of the keyspace using the following command:

```
[default@unknown] SHOW KEYSPACES;
  Durable Writes: true
    Options: [replication_factor:3]
  Column Families:
    ColumnFamily: MyEntries
      Key Validation Class:
      org.apache.cassandra.db.marshal.UTF8Type
      Default column value validator:
      org.apache.cassandra.db.marshal.UTF8Type
      Columns sorted by:
      org.apache.cassandra.db.marshal.ReversedType
      (org.apache.cassandra.db.marshal.TimeUUIDType)
      GC grace seconds: 0
      Compaction min/max thresholds: 4/32
      Read repair chance: 0.1
      DC Local Read repair chance: 0.0
      Replicate on write: true
      Caching: KEYS_ONLY
      Bloom Filter FP chance: default
      Built indexes: []
      Compaction Strategy:
      org.apache.cassandra.db.compaction.
      SizeTieredCompactionStrategy
```

```
Compression Options:
  sstable_compression:
  org.apache.cassandra.io.compress.SnappyCompressor
ColumnFamily: MYDevicesEntries
  Key Validation Class:
  org.apache.cassandra.db.marshal.UUIDType
  Default column value validator:
  org.apache.cassandra.db.marshal.UTF8Type
  Columns sorted by:
  org.apache.cassandra.db.marshal.UTF8Type
  GC grace seconds: 0
  Compaction min/max thresholds: 4/32
  Read repair chance: 0.1
  DC Local Read repair chance: 0.0
  Replicate on write: true
  Caching: KEYS_ONLY
  Bloom Filter FP chance: default
  Built indexes:
  [sidelinedDevicesEntries.
  sidelinedDevicesEntries_date_created_idx,
  sidelinedDevicesEntries.
  sidelinedDevicesEntries_event_type_idx]
  Column Metadata:
    Column Name: event_type
      Validation Class:
      org.apache.cassandra.db.marshal.UTF8Type
      Index Name: sidelinedDevicesEntries_event_type_idx
      Index Type: KEYS
      Index Options: {}
    Column Name: date_created
      Validation Class:
      org.apache.cassandra.db.marshal.DateType
      Index Name: sidelinedDevicesEntries_date_created_idx
      Index Type: KEYS
      Index Options: {}
    Column Name: event
      Validation Class:
      org.apache.cassandra.db.marshal.UTF8Type
  Compaction Strategy:
  org.apache.cassandra.db.compaction.
  SizeTieredCompactionStrategy
  Compression Options:
    sstable_compression:
    org.apache.cassandra.io.compress.SnappyCompressor
```

4. Create a column family:

```
[default@unknown] USE myKeySpace;
  [default@demo] CREATE COLUMN FAMILY appUsers
  WITH comparator = UTF8Type
  AND key_validation_class=UTF8Type
  AND column_metadata = [
  {column_name:user_name, validation_class: UTF8Type}
  {column_name: Dept, validation_class: UTF8Type}
  {column_name: email, validation_class: UTF8Type}
];
```

5. Insert data into the column family:

```
[default@demo] SET appUsers['SS']['user_name']='shilpi';

  [default@demo] SET appUsers['ss']['Dept']='BigData';

  [default@demo] SET
  appUsers['ss']['email']=shilpisaxena@yahoo.com';
```

 In this example, the code ss is my row key.

6. Retrieve data from the Cassandra column family:

```
GET appUsers[utf8('ss')][utf8('user_name')];
List appUsers;
```

Using different client APIs to access Cassandra

Now that we are acquainted with Cassandra, let's move on to the next step where we will access (insert or update) data into the cluster programmatically. In general, the APIs we are talking about are wrappers written over the core Thrift API, which offers various CRUD operations over the Cassandra cluster using programmer-friendly packages.

The client APIs that are used to access Cassandra are as follows:

- **Thrift protocol**: The most basic of all APIs to access Cassandra is the **Remote Procedure Call (RPC)** protocol, which provides a language-neutral interface and thus exposes flexibility to communicate using Python, Java, and so on. Please note that almost all other APIs we'll discuss use **Thrift** under the hood. It is simple to use and it provides basic functionality out of the box like ring discovery and native access. Complex features such as retry, connection pooling, and so on are not supported out of the box. However, there are a variety of libraries that have extended Thrift and added these much required features, and we will touch upon a few widely used ones in this chapter.

- **Hector**: This has the privilege of being one of the most stable and extensively used APIs for Java-based client applications to access Cassandra. As mentioned earlier, it uses Thrift under the hood, so it essentially can't offer any feature or functionality not supported by the Thrift protocol. The reason for its widespread use is that it has a number of essential features ready to use and available out of the box:

    - It has implementation for connection pooling
    - It has a ring discovery feature with an add-on of automatic failover support
    - It has a retry option for downed hosts in the Cassandra ring

- **Datastax Java driver**: This is, again, a recent addition to the stack of client access options to Cassandra, and hence goes well with the newer version of Cassandra. Here are its salient features:

    - Connection pooling
    - Reconnection policies
    - Load balancing
    - Cursor support

- **Astyanax**: This is a very recent addition to the bouquet of Cassandra client APIs and has been developed by Netflix, which definitely makes it more fabled than others. Let's have a look at its credentials to see where it qualifies:

    - It supports all of the functions of Hector and is much easier to use
    - It promises better connection pooling than Hector
    - It is better at handling failovers than Hector
    - It provides some out-of-the-box, database-like features (now that's big news). At the API level, it provides functionality called Recipes in its terms, which provides:

Parallel row query execution

Messaging queue functionality

Object storage

Pagination

° It has numerous frequently required utilities like JSON Writer and CSV Importer

Storm topology wired to the Cassandra store

Now you have been educated and informed about why you should use Cassandra. You have been walked through setting up Cassandra and column family creation, and have even covered the various client/protocol options available to access the Cassandra data store programmatically. As mentioned earlier, Hector has so far been the most widely used API for accessing Cassandra, though the Datastax and Astyanax drivers are fast catching up. For our exercise, we'll use the Hector API.

The use case we want to implement here is to use Cassandra to support real-time, adhoc reporting for telecom data that is being collated, parsed, and enriched using a Storm topology.

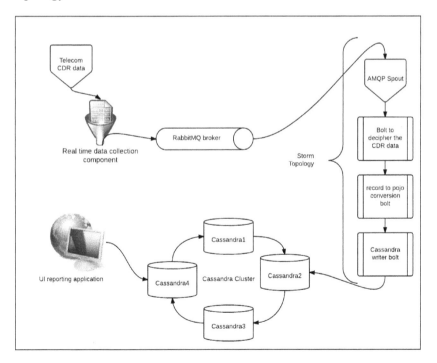

As depicted in the preceding figure, the use case requires live telecom **Call Detail Record (CDR)** capture using the data collection components (for practice, we can use sample records and a simulator shell script to mimic the live CDR feeds). The collated live feed is pushed into the RabbitMQ broker and then consumed by the Storm topology.

For the topology, we have an AMQP spout as the consumer, which reads the data of the queue and pushes it downstream to the topology bolts; here, we have wired in bolts to parse the message and convert it to **Plain Old Java Objects (POJO's)**. Then, we have a new entry in our topology, the Cassandra bolt, which actually stores the data in the Cassandra cluster.

From the Cassandra cluster, a UI-based consumer retrieves the data based on a search query defined by the user, thus providing the adhoc, real-time reporting over live data.

For the sake of our implementation, we will query the data from CLI/CQLSH as shown here:

1. Create a keyspace:

```
create keyspace my_keyspace
  with placement_strategy = 'SimpleStrategy'
  and strategy_options = {replication_factor : 3}
  and durable_writes = true;

use my_keyspace;
```

2. Create the column family:

```
create column family my_columnfamily
  with column_type = 'Standard'
  and comparator = 'UTF8Type'
  and default_validation_class = 'BytesType'
  and key_validation_class = 'TimeUUIDType'
  and read_repair_chance = 0.1
  and dclocal_read_repair_chance = 0.0
  and gc_grace = 0
  and min_compaction_threshold = 4
  and max_compaction_threshold = 32
  and replicate_on_write = true
  and compaction_strategy =
  'org.apache.cassandra.db.compaction.
  SizeTieredCompactionStrategy'
  and caching = 'KEYS_ONLY'
  and bloom_filter_fp_chance = 0.5
  and column_metadata = [
```

```
{column_name : 'cellnumber',
  validation_class : Int32Type },
  {column_name : 'tollchrg',
  validation_class : UTF8Type},
{column_name : 'msgres',
  validation_class : UTF8Type},

{column_name : 'servicetype',
  validation_class : UTF8Type}]
  and compression_options = {'sstable_compression' :
  'org.apache.cassandra.io.compress.SnappyCompressor'
};
```

3. The following changes need to be made to `pom.xml` in the project. The Hector dependency should be added to the `pom.xml` file so that it is fetched at the time of build and added to the `m2` repository, as shown:

```
<dependency>
  <groupId>me.prettyprint</groupId>
  <artifactId>hector-core</artifactId>
  <version>0.8.0-2</version>
</dependency>
```

If you are working with a non-Maven project, follow the usual protocol—download the Hector core JAR file and add it to the project build path so that all the required dependencies are satisfied.

4. Next, we'll need to get the components in place in our Storm topology. We will start by creating a `CassandraController` Java component that will hold all Cassandra-related functionality, and it will be called from the `CassandraBolt` class in the topology to persist the data into Cassandra:

```
public class CassandraController {

    private static final Logger logger =
    LogUtils.getLogger(CassandraManager.class);
    //various serializers are declared in here
    UUIDSerializer timeUUIDSerializer = UUIDSerializer.get();
    StringSerializer stringSerializer =
    StringSerializer.get();
    DateSerializer dateSerializer = DateSerializer.get();
    LongSerializer longSerializer = LongSerializer.get();

    public CassandraController() {
        //list of IPs of Cassandra node in ring
```

```
String nodes =
"10.3.1.41,10.3.1.42,10.3.1.44,10.3.1.45";
String clusterName = "mycluster";
//creating a new configurator
CassandraHostConfigurator hostConfigurator = new
CassandraHostConfigurator(nodes);
hostConfigurator.setCassandraThriftSocketTimeout(0);
cluster = HFactory.getOrCreateCluster(clusterName,
hostConfigurator);

String[] nodeList = nodes.split(",");
if (nodeList != null && nodeList.length ==
cluster.getConnectionManager().
getDownedHosts().size()) {
  logger.error("All cassandra nodes are down. " +
nodes);
}

//setting up read and write consistencies
ConfigurableConsistencyLevel consistency = new
ConfigurableConsistencyLevel();
consistency.setDefaultWriteConsistencyLevel
(HConsistencyLevel.ONE);
consistency.setDefaultReadConsistencyLevel
(HConsistencyLevel.ONE);
keySpaceObj = HFactory.createKeyspace
("my_keyspace", cluster, consistency);
stringMutator = HFactory.createMutator
(keySpaceObj, stringSerializer);
uuidMutator = HFactory.createMutator
(keySpaceObj, timeUUIDSerializer);

logger.info("Cassandra data store initialized,
Nodes=" + nodes + ", " + "cluster name=" +
clusterName + ", " + "keyspace=" + keyspace + ", " +
"consistency=" + writeConsistency);
}
//defining the mutator
public Mutator < Composite > getCompositeMutator() {
  return compositeMutator;
}

public void setCompositeMutator(Mutator < Composite >
compositeMutator) {
    this.compositeMutator = compositeMutator;
```

```
    }
    //getter and setters for all mutators and serializers

  public StringSerializer getStringSerializer() {
    return stringSerializer;
  }

  public Keyspace getKeyspace() {
    return keySpaceObj;
  }
}
```

5. Last but not least in our topology is actually the component that will write into Cassandra, the Storm bolt that will make use of CassandraController created earlier to write the real-time data into Cassandra:

```
public class CassandraBolt extends BaseBasicBolt {
  private static final Logger logger =
  LogUtils.getLogger(CassandraBolt.class);

  public void prepare(Map stormConf, TopologyContext
  context) {

    logger.debug("Cassandra bolt, prepare()");
    try {
      cassandraMngr = new CassandraController();
      myCf = "my_columnfamily";
      );

    } catch (Exception e) {
      logger.error("Error while instantiating
      CassandraBolt", e);
      throw new RuntimeException(e);
    }
  }

  @Override
  public void execute(Tuple input, BasicOutputCollector
  collector) {
    logger.debug("execute method :: Start ");
      Calendar tCalendar = null;
      long eventts = eventObj.getEventTimestampMillis();
      com.eaio.uuid.UUID uuid = new
      com.eaio.uuid.UUID(getTimeForUUID(eventts),
      clockSeqAndNode);
```

```
        java.util.UUID keyUUID =
        java.util.UUID.fromString(uuid.toString());


        /*
        * Persisting to my CF
        */


        try {
          if (keyUUID != null) {
              cassandraMngrTDR.getUUIDMutator().addInsertion(
                  keyUUID,
                  myCf,
                  HFactory.createColumn("eventts",
                      new Timestamp(tCalendar.getTimeInMillis()),
                      -1, cassandraMngr.getStringSerializer(),
                      cassandraMngr.getDateSerializer()));
            }

        cassandraMngrTDR.getUUIDMutator().addInsertion(
          keyUUID,
          myCf,
          HFactory.createColumn("cellnumber",
          eventObj.getCellnumber(), -1,
          cassandraMngr.getStringSerializer(),
            cassandraMngr.getLongSerializer()));
            cassandraMngr.getUUIDMutator().execute();
        logger.debug("CDR event with key = " + keyUUID + "
        inserted into Cassandra cf " + myCf);

        } else {
        logger.error("Record not saved. Error while parsing date
        to generate KEY for cassandra data store, column family -
        " + myCf);
          }
        }

        catch (Exception excep) {
        logger.error("Record not saved. Error while saving data
        to cassandra data store, column family - " + myCf,
        excep);
        }

          logger.debug("execute method :: End ");
        }
    }
```

So here we complete the last piece of the puzzle; we can now stream data into Cassandra using Storm in real time. Once you execute the topology end to end, you can verify the data in Cassandra by using the select or list commands on CLI/CQLSH.

The best practices for Storm/Cassandra applications

When working with distributed applications that have SLAs operating 24/7 with a very high velocity and a miniscule average processing time, certain aspects become extremely crucial to be taken care of:

- Network latency plays a big role in real-time applications and can make or break products, so make a very informed and conscious decision on the placement of various nodes in a data center or across data centers. In such situations, it's generally advisable to keep ping latency at a minimum.

- The replication factor should be around three for Cassandra.

- Compaction should be part of routine Cassandra maintenance.

Quiz time

Q.1. State whether the following statements are true or false:

1. Cassandra is a document-based NoSQL.

2. Cassandra has a single point of failure.

3. Cassandra uses consistent hashing for key distribution.

4. Cassandra works on master-slave architecture.

Q.2. Fill in the blanks:

1. _____attributes of the CAP theorem are adhered to by Cassandra.

2. _____ is the salient feature that makes Cassandra a contender to be used in conjunction with Storm.

3. The _____ is an API to access Cassandra using a Java client, and is a Greek mythological character — *brother of Cassandra*.

Q.3. Complete the use case mentioned in the chapter and demonstrate end-to-end execution to populate data into Cassandra.

Summary

In this chapter, you have covered the fundamentals of NoSQL in general and specifically Cassandra. You got hands-on experience in setting up the Cassandra cluster as well as got to know about varied APIs, drivers, and protocols that provide programmatic access to Cassandra. We also integrated Cassandra as a data store to our Storm topology for data insertion.

In the next chapter, we will touch upon some integral aspects of Cassandra, specifically consistency and availability.

7
Cassandra Partitioning, High Availability, and Consistency

In this chapter, you will understand the internals of Cassandra to learn how data partitioning is implemented and you'll learn about the hashing technique employed on Cassandra's keyset distribution. We will also get an insight into replication and how it works, and the feature of hinted handoff. We will cover the following topics:

- Data partitioning and consistent hashing; we'll look at practical examples
- Replication, consistency, and high availability

Consistent hashing

Before you understand its implication and application in Cassandra, let's understand consistent hashing as a concept.

Consistent hashing works on the concept in its name—that is *hashing* and as we know, for a said hashing algorithm, the same key will always return the same hash code—thus, making the approach pretty deterministic by nature and implementation. When we use this approach for sharding or dividing the keys across the nodes in the cluster, consistent hashing is the technique that determines which node is stored in which node in the cluster.

Have a look at the following diagram to understand the concept of consistent hashing; imagine that the ring depicted in the following diagram represents the Cassandra ring and the nodes are marked here in letters along with the numerals that actually mark the objects (inverted triangles) to be mapped to the ring.

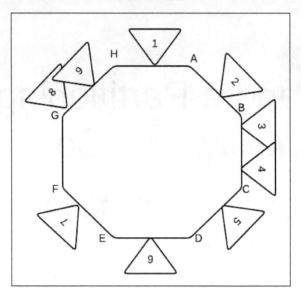

Consistent hashing for the Cassandra cluster

To compute the ownership of the object to the node it belongs to, all that's required is traversal in clockwise to encounter the next node. The node that follows the data item, which is an inverted triangle, is the node that owns the object, for example:

- 1 belongs to node **A**
- 2 belongs to node **B**
- 3 belongs to node **C**
- 4 belongs to node **C**
- 5 belongs to node **D**
- 6 belongs to node **E**
- 7 belongs to node **F**
- 8 belongs to node **H**
- 9 belongs to node **H**

So as you see, this uses simple hashing to compute the ownership of the key in a ring, based on owned token range.

Let's look at a practical example of consistent hashing; to explain this let's take a sample column family where the partition key value is the name.

Let's say the following is the column value data:

Name	Gender
Jammy	M
Carry	F
Jesse	M
Sammy	F

Here is what the hash-mapping would look like:

Partition key	Hash value
Jim	2245462676723220000.00
Carol	7723358927203680000.00
Johnny	6723372854036780000.00
Suzy	1168604627387940000.00

Let's say I have four nodes with the following range; here is how the data would be distributed:

Node	Start range	End range	Partition key	Hash value
A	9223372036854770000.00	4611686018427380000.00	Jammy	6723372854036780000.00
B	4611686018427380000.00	1.00	Jesse	2245462676723220000.00
C	0.00	4611686018427380000.00	suzy	1168604627387940000.00
D	4611686018427380000.00	9223372036854770000.00	Carry	7723358927203680000.00

Now that you understand the concept of consistent hashing, let's look at the scenarios where the one or more node goes down and comes back up.

One or more node goes down

We are currently looking at a very common scenario where we envision that one node goes down; for instance, here we have captured two of them going down: **B** and **E**. What will happen now? Well nothing much, we'd follow the same pattern as before, which moves clockwise to find the next live node and allocate the values to that node.

So in our case, the allocations would change to the following:

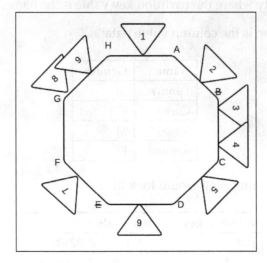

The allocation in the preceding figure is as follows:

- 1 belongs to **A**
- **2**, **3**, and **4** belong to **C**
- 5 belongs to **D**
- **6**, and **7** belong to **F**
- **8**, and **9** belong to **H**

One or more node comes back up

Now let's assume a scenario where node **2** comes back up; well, what happens then is again the same as on prior explanation, and the ownership is reestablished as follows:

- 1 belongs to **A**
- 2 belongs to **B**
- **3**, and **4** belong to **C**
- 5 belongs to **D**
- **6**, and **7** belong to **F**
- **8**, and **9** belong to **H**

So, we have demonstrated that this techniques works for all situations and that's why it is used.

Replication in Cassandra and strategies

Replicating means to create a copy. This copy makes the data redundant and thus available even when one node fails or goes down. In Cassandra, you have the option to specify the replication factor as part of the creation of the keyspace or to later modify it. Attributes that need to be specified in this context are as follows:

- **Replication factor**: This is a numeric value specifying the number of replicas
- **Strategy**: This could be simple strategy or topology strategy; this decides the placement of replicas across the cluster

Internally, Cassandra uses the row key to store replicas or copies of data across various nodes on the cluster. A replication factor of n means there are n copies of data stored on n different nodes. There are certain rules of thumb with replication, and they are as follows:

- A replication factor should never be more than the number of nodes in a cluster, or you will run into exceptions due to not enough replicas and Cassandra will start rejecting the writes and reads, though replication factor would continue uninterrupted
- A replication factor should not be so small that data is lost forever if one odd node goes down

Snitch is used to determine the physical location of nodes, attributes such as closeness to each other, and so on, which are of value when a vast amount of data is to be replicated and moved to and fro. In all such situations, network latency plays a very important part. The two strategies currently supported by Cassandra are as follows:

- **Simple**: This is the default strategy provided by Cassandra for all keyspaces. It employs around a single data center. It's pretty straightforward and simple in its operation; as the name suggests, the partitioner checks the key-value against the node range to determine the placement of the first replica. Thereon, the subsequent replicas are placed on the next nodes in a clockwise order. So if data item "A" has a replication of "3", and the partitioner decides the first node based on the key and ownership, on this node the subsequent replicas are created in a clockwise order.

- **Network**: This is the topology that is used when we have the Cassandra cluster distributed across data centers. Here, we can plan our replica placement and define how many replicas we want to place in each data center. This approach makes the data geo-redundant and thus more fail-safe in cases where the entire data center crashes. The following are two things you should consider when making a choice on replica placement across data centers:

  ○ Each data center should be self-sufficient to satisfy the requests

  ○ Failover or crash situations

If we have 2 *replicas of datum in a data center*, then we have four copies of data and each data center has a tolerance for one node failure for the consistency ONE. If we get into the node of 3 *replicas of datum in a data center*, then we have six copies of data and each data center has a tolerance for multiple node failures for the consistency of ONE. This strategy also permits asymmetrical replication.

Cassandra consistency

As we said in an earlier chapter, Cassandra eventually becomes consistent and follows the AP principal of the CAP theorem. Consistency refers to how up to date the information across all data replicas in a Cassandra cluster is. Cassandra does eventually guarantee consistency. Now let's have a closer look; well, let's say I have five node Cassandra clusters and a replication factor of 3. This means if I have a *data item1*, it would be replicated to three nodes, let's say node1, node2, and node3; let's assume the key of this datum is *key1*. Now if the value of this key is to be rewritten and the write operation is performed on node1, then Cassandra internally replicates the values to other replicas, which are node2 and node3. But this update happens in the background and is not immediate; this is the mechanism of eventual consistency.

Cassandra provides the concept of offering the (read and write) client applications the decision of what consistency level they want to use to read and write to the data store.

Write consistency

Let's inspect the write operation a little closely in Cassandra. Well, when a write operation is done in Cassandra, the client can specify the consistency at which the operation should be performed.

This means that if the replication factor is x and a write operation is performed with a consistency of y (where y is less than x), then Cassandra will wait for successful write to complete on y nodes before returning a successful acknowledgement to the client, marking the operation as complete. For the remaining x-y replicas, the data is propagated and replicated internally by the Cassandra processes.

The following table shows the various consistency levels and their implication where we have ANY that has the benefit of the highest availability with the lowest consistency, and ALL that offers the highest consistency but the lowest availability. So, being a client, one has to review the use case before deciding upon which consistency to choose. The following is a table with a few popular options and their implications:

Consistency level	Implication
ANY	The write operation is returned as successful when the datum is written onto at least one node, where the node could either be a replica node or a non-replica node
ONE	The write operation is returned as successful when the datum is written onto at least one replica node
TWO	The write operation is returned as successful when the datum is written onto at least two replica nodes
QUORUM	The write operation is returned as successful when the datum is written to the quorum of the replica node (where the quorum is n/2+1, and n is the replication factor)
ALL	The write operation is returned as successful when the datum is written onto all replica nodes

The following figure depicting the write operation on a four-node cluster, which has a replication factor of **3** and consistency of **2**:

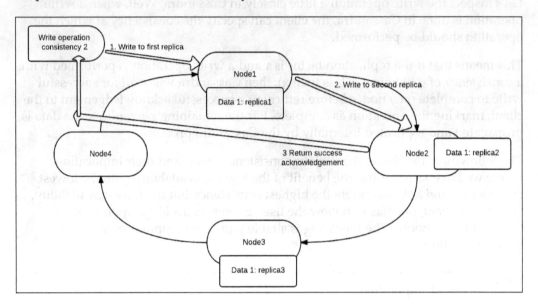

So as you see, the write operation is completed in three steps:

- A write is issued from the client
- The write is executed and completed on **replica1**
- The write is executed and completed on **replica2**
- An acknowledgement is issued to the client when a write is successfully completed

Read consistency

The read consistency is analogues to write consistency, it denotes how many replicas should respond or confirm their alignment to the data being returned to read operation before the results are returned to the client querying the Cassandra data store. This means if on an N node cluster with a replication factor of x, a read query is issued with a read consistency of y (y is less than x), then Cassandra would check the y replicas and then return the results. The results are validated on the basis that the most recent data is used to satisfy the request, and this is verified by the timestamp associated with each column.

The following **Cassandra Query Language** (**CQL**), fetch the data from the column family with quorum consistency as follows:

```
SELECT * FROM mytable USING CONSISTENCY QUORUM WHERE name='shilpi';
```

The functions of the CQL are as follows:

Consistency level	Implication
ONE	A read request is serviced by the response from the closest replica
TWO	A read request is serviced by the most recent response from one of the two closest replicas
THREE	This level returns the most recent data from three of the closest replicas
QUORUM	A read request is serviced by the most recent responses from the quorum of replicas
ALL	A read request is serviced by the most recent response from all the replicas

Consistency maintenance features

In the previous section, we discussed read and write consistency in depth, and one thing that came clear is that Cassandra doesn't provide or work towards total consistency at the time the read or write operation is performed; it executes and completes the request as per client's consistency specifications. Another feature is *eventual consistency*, which highlights that there is some magic behind the veil that guarantees that eventually all data will be consistent. Now this magic is performed by certain components within Cassandra, and some are mentioned as follows:

- **Read repair**: This service ensures that data across all the replicas is and up to date. This way, the row is consistent and has been updated with recent values across all replicas. This operation is executed by a job. Cassandra is running to execute repair read operation issued by the coordinator.

- **Anti-entropy repair service**: This service ensures that the data that's not read very frequently, or when a downed host joins back, is in consistent a state. This is a regular cluster maintenance operation.

- **Hinted handoff**: This is another unique and wonderful operation on Cassandra. When the write operation is executed, the coordinator issues a write operation to all replicas, irrespective of the consistency specified and waits for an acknowledgement. As soon as the acknowledgement count reaches the value mentioned on consistency of the operation, the thread is completed and the client is notified about its success. On the remaining replicas, the values are written using hinted handoffs. The hinted handoff approach is a savior when a few nodes are down. Let's say one of the replicas is down and a write operation is executed with a consistency of ANY; in that case, one replica takes the write operation and hints to the neighboring replicas, which are currently down. When the downed replicas are revived, then the values are written back to them by taking hints from live replicas.

Quiz time

Q.1. State whether the following statements are true or false:

1. Cassandra has a default consistency of ALL.
2. QUORUM is the consistency level that provides the highest availability.
3. Cassandra uses a snitch to identify the closeness of the nodes.
4. Cassandra reads and writes features have consistency level 1 by default.

Q.2. Fill in the blanks:

1. _____ is used to determine the physical closeness of the nodes.
2. _____ is the consistency that provides the highest availability and lowest availability.
3. The _____ is the service that ensures that a node, which has been down for a while, is correctly updated with the latest changes.

Q.3. Execute the following use case to see Cassandra high availability and replications:

1. Create a four-node Cassandra cluster.
2. Create a keyspace with a replication factor of 3.
3. Add some data into a column family under this keyspace.
4. Attempt to retrieve data using read consistency with using ALL in select query.
5. Shut down the Cassandra daemon on one node and repeat step 4 from the other three live nodes.
6. Shut down the Cassandra daemon on one node and repeat step 4 from the other three live nodes using the consistency ANY.

7. Shut down two nodes and update an existing value using a write consistency of ANY.

8. Attempt a read using ANY.

9. Bring back the nodes that are down and execute read using the consistency ALL from all four nodes.

Summary

In this chapter, you have understood the concepts of replication and data partitioning in Cassandra. We also understood the replication strategy and the concept of eventual consistency. The exercise at the end of the chapter is a good hands-on exercise to help you understand the concepts covered in the chapter in a practical way.

In the next chapter, we will discuss the gossip protocols, Cassandra cluster maintenance, and management features.

8
Cassandra Management and Maintenance

In this chapter, we will learn about the gossip protocol of Cassandra. Thereafter, we will delve into Cassandra administration and management in terms of understanding scaling and reliability in action. This will equip you with the ability to handle situations that you would not like to come across but do happen in production, such as handling recoverable nodes, rolling restarts, and so on.

The topics that will be covered in the chapter are as follows:

- Cassandra—gossip protocol
- Cassandra scaling—adding a new node to a cluster
- Replacing a node
- Replication factor changes
- Node tool commands
- Rolling restarts and fault tolerance
- Cassandra monitoring tools

So, this chapter will help you understand the basics of Cassandra, as well as the various options required for the maintenance and management of Cassandra activities.

Cassandra – gossip protocol

Gossip is a protocol wherein periodically the nodes exchange information with other nodes about the nodes they know; this way, all the nodes obtain information about each other via this peer-to-peer communication mechanism. It's very similar to real-world and social media world gossip.

Cassandra executes this mechanism every second, and one node is capable of exchanging gossip information with up to three nodes in the cluster. All these gossip messages have a version associated with them to track the chronology, and the older gossip interaction updates are overwritten chronologically by newer ones.

Now that we know what Cassandra's gossip is like at a very high level, let's have a closer look at it and understand the purpose of this chatty protocol. Here are the two broad purposes served by having this in place:

- Bootstrapping
- Failure scenario handling – detection and recovery

Let's understand what they mean in action and what their contribution is towards the well-being and stability of a Cassandra cluster.

Bootstrapping

Bootstrapping is a process that is triggered in a cluster when a node joins the ring for the first time. It's the seed nodes that we define under the `Cassandra.yaml` configuration file that help the new nodes obtain the information about the cluster, ring, keyset, and partition ranges. It's recommended that you keep the setting similar throughout the cluster; otherwise, you could run into partitions within the cluster. A node remembers which nodes it has gossiped with even after it restarts. One more point to remember about seed nodes is that their purpose is to serve the nodes at the time of bootstrap; beyond this, its neither a single point of failure, nor does it serve any other purpose.

Failure scenario handling – detection and recovery

Well, the gossip protocol is Cassandra's own efficient way of knowing when a failure has occurred; that is, the entire ring gets to know about a downed host through gossip. On a contrary, situation when a node joins the cluster, the same mechanism is employed to inform the all nodes in the ring.

Once Cassandra detects a failure of a nodes on the ring, it stops routing the client requests to it—failure definitely has some impact on the overall performance of the cluster. However, it's never a blocker until we have enough replicas for consistency to be served to the client.

Another interesting fact about gossip is that it happens at various levels—Cassandra gossip, like real-world gossip, could be secondhand or thirdhand and so on; this is the manifestation of indirect gossip.

Failure of a node could be actual or virtual. This means that either a node can actually fail due to system hardware giving away, or the failure could be virtual, wherein, for a while, network latency is so high that it would seem that the node is not responding. The latter scenarios, most of the time, are self-recoverable; that is, after a while, networks return to normalcy, and the nodes are detected in the ring once again. The live nodes keep trying to ping and gossip with the failed node periodically to see if they are up. If a node is to be declared as permanently departed from the cluster, we require some admin intervention to explicitly remove the node from the ring.

When a node is joined back to the cluster after quite a while, it's possible that it might have missed a couple of writes (inserts/updates/deletes), and thus, the data on the node is far from being accurate as per the latest state of data. It's advisable to run a repair using the `nodetool repair` command.

Cassandra cluster scaling – adding a new node

Cassandra scales very easily, and with zero downtime. This is one of the reasons why it is chosen over many other contenders. The steps are pretty straightforward and simple:

1. You need to set up Cassandra on the nodes to be added. Don't start the Cassandra process yet; first, follow these steps:

    1. Update the seed nodes in `Cassandra.yaml` under `seed_provider`.

    2. Make sure the `tmp` folders are clean.

    3. Add `auto_bootstrap` to `Cassandra.yaml` and set it to `true`.

    4. Update `cluster_name` in `Cassandra.yaml`.

    5. Update `listen_address/broadcast_address` in `Cassandra.yaml`.

2. Start all the new nodes one by one, pausing for at least 5 minutes between two consecutive starts.

3. Once the node is started, it will proclaim its share of data based on the token range it owns and start streaming that in. This could be verified using the `nodetoolnetstat` command, as shown in the following code:

```
mydomain@my-cass1:/home/ubuntu$ /usr/local/cassandra/apache-
   cassandra-1.1.6/bin/nodetool -h 10.3.12.29 netstats | grep -
   v 0%
Mode: JOINING
Not sending any streams.
Streaming from: /10.3.12.179
my_keyspace:
   /var/lib/cassandra/data/my_keyspace/mycf/my_keyspace-my-hf-
   461279-Data.db sections=1
   progress=2382265999194/3079619547748 - 77%
Pool Name                    Active      Pending         Completed
Commands                        n/a            0                33
Responses                       n/a            0          13575829
mydomain@my-cass1:/home/ubuntu$
```

4. After all the nodes are joined to the cluster, it's strictly recommended that you run a `nodetool cleanup` command on all the nodes. This is recommended so that they relinquish the control of the keys that were formerly owned by them but now belong to the new nodes that have joined the cluster. Here is the command and the execution output:

```
mydomain@my-cass3:/usr/local/cassandra/apache-cassandra-
   1.1.6/bin$ sudo -bE ./nodetool -h 10.3.12.178 cleanup
   my_keyspacemycf_index
mydomain@my-cass3:/usr/local/cassandra/apache-cassandra-
   1.1.6/bin$ du -h
   /var/lib/cassandra/data/my_keyspace/mycf_index/
53G  /var/lib/cassandra/data/my_keyspace/mycf_index/
mydomain@my-cass3:/usr/local/cassandra/apache-cassandra-
   1.1.6/bin$ jps
27389 Jps
26893 NodeCmd
17925 CassandraDaemon
```

5. Note that the `NodeCmd` process is actually the cleanup process for the Cassandra daemon. The disk space reclaimed after the cleanup on the preceding node is shown here:

```
Size before cleanup - 57G
Size after cleanup - 30G
```

Cassandra cluster – replacing a dead node

This section captures the various situations and scenarios that can occur and cause failures in a Cassandra cluster. We will also equip you with the knowledge and talk about the steps to handle these situations. These situations are specific to version 1.1.6 but can be applied to others as well.

Say, this is the problem: you're running an n node, for example let's say there are three node clusters and from that one node goes down; this will result in unrecoverable hardware failure. The solution is this: replace the dead nodes with new nodes.

The following are the steps to achieve the solution:

1. Confirm the node failure using the `nodetool ring` command:

    ```
    bin/nodetool ring -h hostname
    ```

2. The dead node will be shown as DOWN; let's assume node3 is down:

    ```
    192.168.1.54 datacenter1rack1 Up   Normal 755.25 MB 50.00% 0
    ```

    ```
    192.168.1.55 datacenter1rack1 Down Normal 400.62 MB 25.00%
       42535295865117307932921825928971026432
    ```

    ```
    192.168.1.56 datacenter1rack1 Up   Normal 793.06 MB 25.00%
       85070591730234615865843651857942052864
    ```

3. Install and configure Cassandra on the replacement node. Make sure we remove the old installation, if any, from the replaced Cassandra node using the following command:

    ```
    sudorm -rf /var/lib/cassandra/*
    ```

    Here, `/var/lib/cassandra` is the path of the Cassandra data directory for Cassandra.

4. Configure `Cassandra.yaml` so that it holds the same non-default settings as that of the pre-existing Cassandra cluster.

5. Set the `initial_token` range in the `cassandra.yaml` file of the replacement node to the value of the dead node's token 1, that is, `42535295865117307932 921825928971026431`.

6. Starting the new node will join the cluster at one place prior to the dead node in the ring:

    ```
    192.168.1.54 datacenter1rack1 Up    Normal 755.25 MB 50.00% 0
    192.168.1.51 datacenter1rack1 Up    Normal 400.62 MB 0.00%
       42535295865117307932921825928971026431
    ```

```
192.168.1.55 datacenter1rack1 Down     Normal 793.06 MB 25.00%
   42535295865117307932921825928971026432

192.168.1.56 datacenter1rack1 Up      Normal 793.06 MB 25.00%
   85070591730234615865843651857942052864
```

7. We are almost done. Just run `nodetool repair` on each node on each keyspace:

```
nodetool repair -h 192.168.1.54 keyspace_name -pr
nodetool repair -h 192.168.1.51 keyspace_name -pr
nodetool repair -h 192.168.1.56 keyspace_name-pr
```

8. Remove the token of the dead node from the ring using the following command:

```
nodetoolremovetoken 85070591730234615865843651857942052864
```

This command needs to be executed on all the remaining nodes to make sure all the live nodes know that the dead node is no longer available.

9. This removes the dead node from the cluster; now we are done.

The replication factor

Occasionally, there are instances when we come across situations where we make changes to the replication factor. For example, I started with a smaller cluster so I kept my replication factor as 2. Later, I scaled out from 4 nodes to 8 nodes, and thus to make my entire setup more fail-safe, I increased my replication factor to 4. In such situations, the following steps are to be followed:

1. The following is the command to update the replication factor and/or change the strategy. Execute these commands on the Cassandra CLI:

```
ALTER KEYSPACEmy_keyspace WITH REPLICATION = { 'class' :
  'SimpleStrategy', 'replication_factor' : 4 };
```

2. Once the command has been updated, you have to execute the `nodetool` repair on each of the nodes one by one (in succession) so that all the keys are correctly replicated as per the new replication values:

```
sudo -bE ./nodetool -h 10.3.12.29 repair my_keyspacemycf -pr
6
mydomain@my-cass3:/home/ubuntu$ sudo -E
  /usr/local/cassandra/apache-cassandra-1.1.6/bin/nodetool -h
  10.3.21.29 compactionstats
pending tasks: 1
compaction type  keyspace          column family bytes
  compacted        bytes total  progress
```

```
Validation        my_keyspacemycf   1826902206
   761009279707    0.24%
Active compaction remaining time :          n/a
mydomain@my-cass3:/home/ubuntu$
```

The following `compactionstats` command is used to track the progress of the `nodetool repair` command.

The nodetool commands

The `nodetool` command in Cassandra is the most handy tool in the hands of a Cassandra administrator. It has all the tools and commands that are required for all types of situational handling of various nodes. Let's look at a few widely used ones closely:

- `Ring`: This command depicts the state of nodes (normal, down, leaving, joining, and so on). The ownership of the token range and percentage ownership of the keys along with the data centre and rack details is as follows:

  ```
  bin/nodetool -host 192.168.1.54 ring
  ```

  The output will be something like this:

  ```
  192.168.1.54 datacenter1rack1 Up    Normal 755.25 MB 50.00% 0
  192.168.1.51 datacenter1rack1 Up    Normal 400.62 MB 0.00%
     42535295865117307932921825928971026431
  192.168.1.55 datacenter1rack1 Down  Normal 793.06 MB 25.00%
     42535295865117307932921825928971026432
  192.168.1.56 datacenter1rack1 Up    Normal 793.06 MB 25.00%
     85070591730234615865843651857942052864
  ```

- `Join`: This is the option you can use with `nodetool`, which needs to be executed to add the new node to the cluster. When a new node joins the cluster, it starts streaming the data from other nodes until it receives all the keys as per its designated ownership based on the token in the ring. The status for this can be checked using the `netsat` commands:

  ```
  mydomain@my-cass3:/home/ubuntu$ /usr/local/cassandra/apache-
     cassandra-1.1.6/bin/nodetool -h 10.3.12.29 netstats | grep -
     v 0%
  Mode: JOINING
  Not sending any streams.
  Streaming from: /10.3.12.179
  ```

```
my_keyspace:
/var/lib/cassandra/data/my_keyspace/mycf/my_keyspace-mycf-
hf-46129-Data.db sections=1
progress=238226599194/307961954748 - 77%
Pool Name                      Active    Pending       Completed
Commands                          n/a          0              33
Responses                         n/a          0        13575829
```

- Info: This nodetool option gets all the required information about the node specified in the following command:

```
bin/nodetool -host 10.176.0.146 info
Token(137462771597874153173150284137310597304)
Load Info        : 0 bytes.
Generation No    : 1
Uptime (seconds) : 697595
Heap Memory (MB) : 28.18 / 759.81
```

- Cleanup: This is the option that is generally used when we scale the cluster. New nodes are added and thus the existing nodes need to relinquish the control of the keys that now belong to the new entrants in the cluster:

```
mydomain@my-cass3:/usr/local/cassandra/apache-cassandra-
   1.1.6/bin$ sudo -bE ./nodetool -h 10.3.12.178 cleanup
   my_keyspacemycf_index
mydomain@my-cass3:/usr/local/cassandra/apache-cassandra-
   1.1.6/bin$ du -h
   /var/lib/cassandra/data/my_keyspace/mycf_index/
53G  /var/lib/cassandra/data/my_keyspace/mycf_index/
aeris@nrt-prod-cass3-C2:/usr/local/cassandra/apache-cassandra-
   1.1.6/bin$ sudo `which jps
27389 Jps
26893 NodeCmd
17925 CassandraDaemon
mydomain@my-cass3:/usr/local/cassandra/apache-cassandra-
   1.1.6/bin$ du -h
   /var/lib/cassandra/data/my_keyspace/mycf_index/
53G  /var/lib/cassandra/data/my_keyspace/mycf_index/
```

- Compaction: This is one of the most useful tools. It's used to explicitly issue the compact command to Cassandra. This can be done on the entire node, key space, or at the column family level:

```
sudo -bE /usr/local/cassandra/apache-cassandra-
   1.1.6/bin/nodetool -h 10.3.1.24 compact
```

```
mydomain@my-cass3:/home/ubuntu$ sudo -E
  /usr/local/cassandra/apache-cassandra-1.1.6/bin/nodetool -h
  10.3.1.24 compactionstats
pending tasks: 1
compaction type keyspace column family bytes compacted bytes
  total progress
Compaction my_keyspacemycf 1236772 1810648499806 0.00%
Active compaction remaining time:29h58m42s
mydomain@my-cass3:/home/ubuntu$
```

Cassandra has two types of compactions: minor compaction and major compaction. The minor cycle of compaction gets executed whenever a new `sstable` data is created to remove all the tombstones (that is, the deleted entries).

The major compaction is something that's triggered manually, using the preceding `nodetool` command. This can be applied to the node, keyspace, and a column family level.

- `Decommission`: This is, in a way, the opposite of bootstrap and is triggered when we want a node to leave the cluster. The moment a live node receives the command, it stops accepting new rights, flushes the `memtables`, and starts streaming the data from itself to the nodes that would be a new owner of the key range it currently owns:

  ```
  bin/nodetool -h 192.168.1.54 decommission
  ```

- `Removenode`: This command is executed when a node is dead, that is, physically unavailable. This informs the other nodes about the node being unavailable. Cassandra replication kicks into action to restore the correct replication by creating copies of data as per the new ring ownership:

  ```
  bin/nodetoolremovenode<UUID>
  bin/nodetoolremovenode force
  ```

- `Repair`: This `nodetool repair` command is executed to fix the data on any node. This is a very important tool to ensure that there is data consistency and the nodes that join the cluster back after a period of time exist. Let's assume a cluster with four nodes that are catering to continuous writes through a storm topology. Here, one of the nodes goes down and joins the ring again after an hour or two. Now, during this duration, the node might have missed some writes; to fix this data, we should execute a `repair` command on the node:

  ```
  bin/nodetool repair
  ```

Cassandra fault tolerance

Well, one of the prime reasons for using Cassandra as a data store is its fault-tolerant capabilities. It's not driven by a typical master-slave architecture, where failure of the master becomes a single point of system breakdown. Instead, it harbors a concept of operating in a ring mode so that there is no single point of failure. Whenever required, we can restart the nodes without the dread of bringing the whole cluster down; there are various situations where this capability comes in handy.

There are situations where we need to restart Cassandra, but Cassandra's ring architecture equips the administrator to do this seamlessly with zero downtime for the cluster. This means that in situations such as the following that requires a Cassandra cluster to be restarted, a Cassandra administrator can restart the nodes one by one instead of bringing down the entire cluster and then starting it:

- Starting the Cassandra daemon with changes in the memory configuration
- Enabling JMX on an already running Cassandra cluster
- Sometimes machines have routine maintenance and need restarts

Cassandra monitoring systems

Now that we have discussed the various management aspects of Cassandra, let's explore the various dashboarding and monitoring options for the Cassandra cluster. There are various free and licensed tools available that we'll discuss now.

JMX monitoring

You can use a type of monitoring for Cassandra that is based on `jconsole`. Here are the steps to connect to Cassandra using `jconsole`:

1. In the Command Prompt, execute the `jconsole` command:

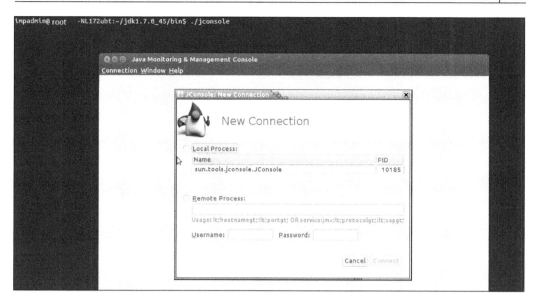

2. In the next step, you have to specify the Cassandra node IP and port for connectivity:

3. Once you are connected, JMX provides a variety of graphs and monitoring utilities:

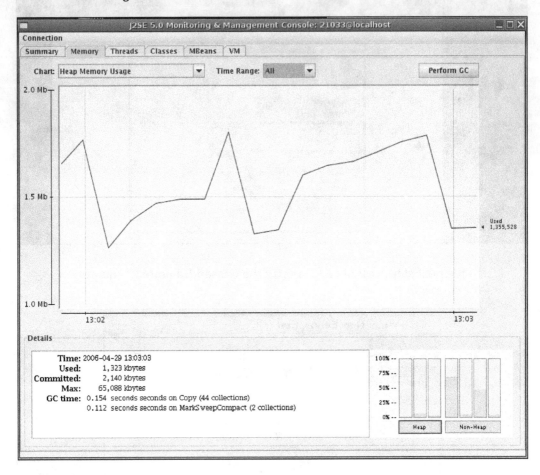

The developers can monitor heap memory usage using the jconsole **Memory** tab. This will help you understand the utilization of node resources.

The limitation with jconsole is that it performs node-specific monitoring and not Cassandra-ring-based monitoring and dashboarding. Let's explore the other tools in the context.

Datastax OpsCenter

This is a datastax-provided utility with a graphical interface that lets the user monitor and execute administrative activities from one central dashboard. Note that a free version is available only for nonproduction usage.

Datastax Ops center provides a lot of graphical representations for various important system **Key Performance Indicators** (**KPIs**), such as performance trends, summary, and so on. Its UI also provides a historic data analysis and drill down capability on single data points. OpsCenter stores all its metrics in Cassandra itself. The key features of the OpsCenter utility are as follows:

- KPI-based monitoring for the entire cluster
- Alerts and alarms
- Configuration management
- Easy to set up

You can install and set up OpsCenter using the following simple steps:

1. Run the following command to get started:

   ```
   $ sudo service opscenterd start
   ```

2. Connect to OpsCenter in a web browser at `http://localhost:8888`.

3. You will get a welcome screen where you will have options to spawn a new cluster or connect to an existing one.

4. Next, configure the agent; once this is done, OpsCenter is ready for use.

Here is a screenshot from the application:

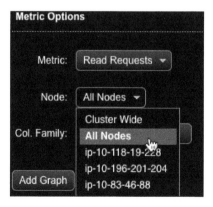

Here we choose the metric to be executed and whether the operation is to be performed on a specific node or all the nodes. The following screenshot captures OpsCenter starting up and recognizing the various nodes in the cluster:

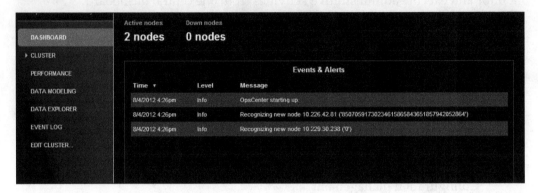

The following screenshot captures various KPIs in the aspects of read and writes to the cluster, the overall cluster latency, disk I/O, and so on:

Quiz time

Q.1. State whether the following statements are true or false.

1. Cassandra has a single point of failure.
2. A dead node is immediately detected in a Cassandra ring.
3. Gossip is a data exchange protocol.
4. The decommission and removenode commands are same.

Q.2. Fill in the blanks.

1. _____ is the command used to run compactions.
2. _____ is the command to get the information about a live node.
3. _____ is the command that displays the entire cluster information.

Q.3. Execute the following use case to see Cassandra high availability and replications:

1. Creating a 4-node Cassandra cluster.
2. Creating a keyspace with a replication factor of 3.
3. Bringing down a Cassandra daemon on one the nodes.
4. Executing `nestat` on each node to see the data streaming.

Summary

In this chapter, you learned about the concepts of the gossip protocol and adapted tools used for various scenarios such as scaling the cluster, replacing a dead node, compaction, and repair operations on Cassandra.

In the next chapter, we will discuss storm cluster maintenance and operational aspects.

9
Storm Management and Maintenance

In this chapter, you will understand scaling of the Storm cluster. You will also see how to adapt the Storm topology worker and parallelism.

We will cover the following topics:

- Adding new supervisor nodes
- Setting up workers and parallelism to enhance processing
- Troubleshooting

Scaling the Storm cluster – adding new supervisor nodes

In production, one of the most common scenarios one can run into is when the processing need outgrows the size of the cluster. Scaling then becomes necessary; there are two options: we can perform vertical scaling wherein we can add more compute capability, or we can use horizontal scaling where we add more nodes. The latter is more cost-effective and also makes the cluster more robust.

Here are the steps to be executed to add a new node to the Storm cluster:

1. Download and install the 0.9.2 version of Storm as it is used in the rest of the cluster by extracting the downloaded ZIP file.
2. Create the required directories:

```
sudo mkdir -p /usr/local/storm/tmp
```

3. All Storm nodes, the Nimbus nodes, and the supervisor require a location on to store a small amount of data related to configurations on the local disk. Please ensure you create the directory and assign read/write permissions on all Storm nodes.

4. Create the required directories for the logs, as follows:

```
sudo mkdir -p /mnt/app_logs/storm/storm_logs
```

5. Update the `storm.yaml` file with necessary changes for Nimbus and Zookeeper:

```
#storm.zookeeper.servers: This is a list of the hosts in the
   Zookeeper cluster for Storm cluster
storm.zookeeper.servers:
   - "<IP_ADDRESS_OF_ZOOKEEPER_ENSEMBLE_NODE_1>"
   - "<IP_ADDRESS_OF_ZOOKEEPER_ENSEMBLE_NODE_2>"
#storm.zookeeper.port: Port on which zookeeper cluster is running.
   storm.zookeeper.port: 2182
#For our installation, we are going to create this directory in
   /usr/local/storm/tmp location.
storm.local.dir: "/usr/local/storm/tmp"
#nimbus.host: The nodes need to know which machine is the #master
   in order to download topology jars and confs. This #property is
   used for the same purpose.
nimbus.host: "<IP_ADDRESS_OF_NIMBUS_HOST>"
#storm.messaging.netty configurations: Storm's Netty-based
   #transport has been overhauled to significantly improve
   #performance through better utilization of thread, CPU, and
   #network resources, particularly in cases where message sizes
   #are small. In order to provide netty support, following
   #configurations need to be added :
storm.messaging.transport:"backtype.storm.messaging.netty.Context"
storm.messaging.netty.server_worker_threads:1
storm.messaging.netty.client_worker_threads:1
storm.messaging.netty.buffer_size:5242880
storm.messaging.netty.max_retries:100
storm.messaging.netty.max_wait_ms:1000
storm.messaging.netty.min_wait_ms:100
```

The values of the slots of the supervisor ports are as follows:

supervisor.slots.ports
- 6700
- 6701
- 6702
- 6703

6. Set the `STORM_HOME` environment in the `~/.bashrc` file and add Storm's `bin` directory in the `PATH` environment variable. This is added to execute Storm binaries from any location. The entry to be added is as follows:

   ```
   STORM_HOME=/usr/local/storm
   PATH=$PATH:$STORM_HOME/bin
   ```

7. Update `/etc/hosts` on each of the following machines and the node:

   ○ The nimbus machine: This is done to add an entry for the new supervisor that's being added

   ○ All existing supervisor machines: This is done to add an entry for the new supervisor that's being added

   ○ The new supervisor node: This is done to add the nimbus entry, to add the entry for all other supervisors, and to add an entry for the Zookeeper node

Here is a sample snippet for the IP 10.46.205.248 and the `sup-flm-1.mydomain.com` host:

```
10.192.206.160    sup-flm-2. mydomain.net
10.4.27.405       nim-zkp-flm-3. mydomain.net
```

Once the supervisor has been added, start the process and it should be visible on the UI, as shown in the following screenshot:

Supervisor summary

Id	Host	Uptime	Slots	Used slots
005fc1b7-e9cc-4103-8644-04b1b024a55d	nrt-prod2-sup1.net	6d 0h 4m 11s	16	0
52fd6480-8774-492a-8373-6c611bd0b286	nrt-prod2-sup3.net	12d 11h 6m 45s	16	15
5c47abb4-e496-497a-91ad-da83c1db034c	nrt-prod2-sup5.net	12d 11h 4m 52s	16	15
799ed64f-01c2-4ae5-ae75-63a97ea2bb18	nrt-prod2-sup6.net	12d 11h 4m 16s	16	14
ced64c18-08ba-4665-a378-31950 7d5fae8	nrt-prod2-sup7.net	12d 11h 3m 53s	16	14
d77f31d5-09cc-4841-a0d7-01a569cb9ac3	nrt-prod2-sup2.net	12d 11h 7m 43s	16	14
e2e1b70a-daf8-4581-92f0-dc47864b5a4e	nrt-prod2-sup4.net	12d 11h 5m 57s	16	15

Note that the first row in the preceding screenshot points to the newly added supervisor; it has 16 slots in total and 0 slots are being used as it has been just added to the cluster.

Scaling the Storm cluster and rebalancing the topology

Once a new supervisor is added, the next obvious step would be to rebalance the topologies, which are executed on the cluster so that the load could be shared across to the newly added supervisor.

Rebalancing using the GUI

Rebalance option is available on the Nimbus UI where you can choose the topology that is to be rebalanced, and then use the option from the GUI. The topology drains as per the specified time-out. During that duration, it stops accepting any messages from the spout and the ones in the internal queues are processed and once completely clear, the workers and tasks are redistributed. The user also has option to increase or decrease the parallelism for various bolts and spouts using the rebalance options. The following screenshot describes how to rebalance a topology using the Storm UI options:

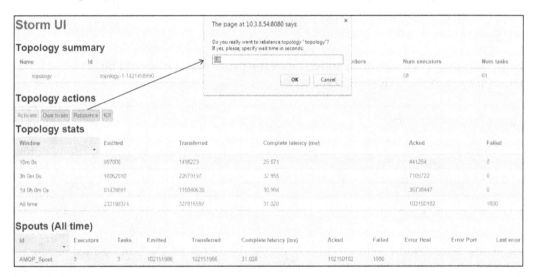

Rebalancing using the CLI

The second option for rebalancing is using the Storm CLI. The command for this is as follows:

```
storm rebalance mystormtopology -n 5 -e my-spout=3 -e my-bolt=10
```

Here, -n specifies the number of workers allocated to the topology post-rebalance, -e my-spout refers to parallelism assigned to the spout, and similarly -e my-bolt refers to parallelism to be assigned to the bolt. In the preceding command, we executed the Storm shell from the `bin` directory under the Storm installation JAR, and while rebalancing the Storm topology by changing the parallelism of the spout and bolts as well.

The changes to the execution of the preceding commands can be verified from the Storm UI.

Setting up workers and parallelism to enhance processing

Storm is a highly scalable, distributed, and fault tolerant real-time parallel processing compute framework. Note that the emphasis is on scalability, distributed, and parallel processing — well, we already know that Storm operates in clustered mode and is therefore distributed in its basic nature. Scalability was covered in the previous section; now, let's have a closer look at parallelism. We introduced you to this concept in an earlier chapter, but now we'll get you acquainted with how to tweak it to achieve the desired performance. The following points are the key criteria for this:

- A topology is allocated a certain number of workers at the time it's started.
- Each component in the topology (bolts and spouts) has a specified number of executors associated with it. These executors specify the number or degree of parallelism for each running component of the topology.
- The whole efficiency and speed factor of Storm are driven by the parallelism feature of Storm, but we need to understand one thing: all the executors that attribute to parallelism are running within the limited set of workers allocated to the topology. So, one needs to understand that increasing the parallelism would help achieve efficiency only to a point, but beyond that the executors will struggle for resource is the intention. Going beyond this increasing parallelism would not fetch efficiency, but increasing the workers allocated to the topology would would make computation efficient.

Another point to understand in terms of efficiency is network latency; we'll explore this in the following sections.

Scenario 1

This following figure illustrates a simple topology with three moving components: one spout and two bolts. Here, all the components are executing on separate nodes in the cluster, thus every tuple has to do two network hops to complete its execution.

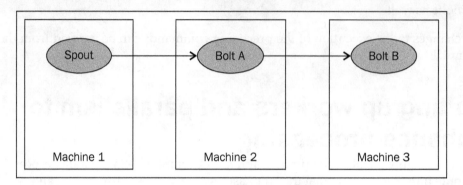

Let's say we are not satisfied with the throughput and decide to increase the parallelism. The moment we try to move into this technique, the question that arises is where to increase it and by how much. That could be computed based on the capacity of the bolt, which should be visible from the Storm UI. The following screenshot illustrates this:

Bolts (All time)						
Id	Executors	Tasks	Emitted	Transferred	Capacity (last 10m)	Execute latency (ms)
cassandra_bolt	3	3	0	0	0.000	8.130
alert_bolt	3	3	5040	5040	0.952	13.505
cass_bolt	2	2	0	0	0.050	3.046
ps_bolt	2	2	2807660	2807660	0.002	0.107
parser_bolt	2	2	72860	218580	0.214	38.611
device_bolt	2	2	0	0	0.019	2.322

Here, the circled value is the capacity of the second bolt, which is around 0.9 and it's already in red, which means this bolt is over-worked and increasing parallelism here should help. Any topology would actually break and stop acking when the bolt capacity crosses 1. To fix this, let's see the next scenario, which provides a solution for this issue.

Scenario 2

Here, we have acted on the realization that **Bolt B** is overloaded and has increased the parallelism, as shown in the following figure:

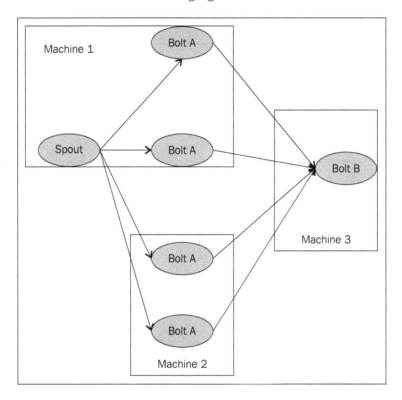

The preceding figure describes one scenario capturing the distribution of various instances of the bolts and spouts across different nodes in the cluster. Here, we have acted on the realization that a bolt is overloaded and we observed the capacity, and by brute force, increased the parallelism of only that bolt.

Now, having done this, we have achieved the required parallelism; let's now have a look at the network latency, in terms of how many tuples are moving between nodes (internode communication is a mandatory element in a distributed computing setup):

- 50 percent of the traffic is hopping between spouts on **Machine 1** and **Machine 2**
- 50 percent of the traffic is hopping between **Machine 1** and **Machine 3**
- 100 percent of the traffic is hopping between **Machine 2** and **Machine 3**

Now let's see another illustration with a slight variation in the parallelism.

Scenario 3

The scenario 3 is the most optimal scenario that is possible in the setup in the example where we use network and parallelism very efficiently, as shown in the following figure:

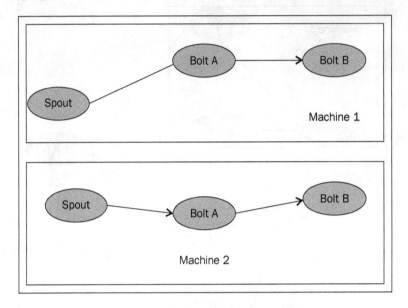

Now, the preceding figure is an illustration of where we get the maximum benefit of parallelism usage. If you look at the preceding figure, you'll see that we have achieved efficiency and no network hop; the best of both the worlds.

What I am trying to illustrate is that parallelism should be changed judicially keeping the impact of network latency, hops, and the speed of localized processing in mind.

Storm troubleshooting

As developers, we need to accept the reality that things do go wrong and debugging is required. This section is going to equip you to handle such situations effectively and efficiently. The first thing is to understand two root mantras of the programming world:

* Work as if everything that could break will break
* Anything that could break can be fixed

Having accepted the reality, let's address the situation first by understanding what could fail and then have a clear understanding of where we should start the analysis to help us handle any situation with the Storm cluster. Let's get to grips with the various pointers that show us the problems and thus guide us to prospective solutions.

The Storm UI

First of all, let's understand which statistics and indicators are present on the UI itself. The latest UI has scores of indicators that give us an insight into what is going on in the cluster and what could go wrong (just in case things break).

Let's look at Storm UI where the **Cluster Summary** entails, for example, `http:// ip of nimbus:8080` in my case is `http://10.4.2.122:8080` and my UI process executes on the nimbus machine that has this IP: 10.4.2.122.

Storm UI

Cluster Summary

Version	Nimbus uptime	Supervisors	Used slots	Free slots	Total slots	Executors	Tasks
0.9.3	8h 14m 6s	6	51	13	64	406	420

In the preceding screenshot, we can see the following parameters:

- The version of Storm being used is in the first column.
- The uptime of Nimbus (second column) tells us how long the Nimbus node has been running since the last restart. Nimbus, as we know, is required only at the time when the topology is submitted or when a supervisor or worker has gone down and the tasks are being delegated again. Nimbus is also required to be up during the rebalancing of the topology.
- The third column gives us the number of supervisors on the cluster.
- Columns four, five, and six show the number of used worker slots, number of free worker slots, and total number of worker slots across the Storm supervisors. This is a very important statistic. In any production grade cluster, one should always have a provision for some of the workers going down or one or two supervisors being killed. So, I recommend that you always have enough free slots on your cluster to accommodate such sudden failures.
- Column seven and column eight specify the moving tasks in the topology, that is, in terms of the number of tasks and executors running in the system.

Let's have a look at the second section on the Storm UI opening page; this one captures the topology summary:

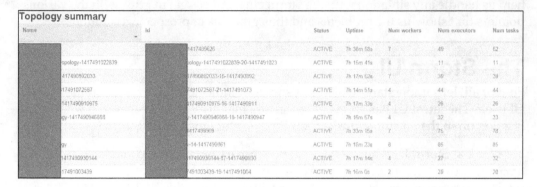

This section depicts various parameters Storm captures and displays at the topology level:

- Column one and column two display the **Name** field of the topology and the **Id** field of topology, respectively.

- Column three reads the status of the topology, which is **ACTIVE** for a topology that's executing and processing.

- Column four displays the uptime since the topology has been started.

- The next three columns display **Numworkers**, **Num tasks**, and **Num executors**; these are very important aspects for the performance of the topology. While tuning the performance, one has to realize that just increasing the **Num tasks** and **Num executors** field value may not result in greater efficiency. If the number of workers is low, and we just increase the number of executors and tasks, then the starvation of resource high because of the limited number of workers, so the topology performance will deteriorate.

Similarly, if we assign too many workers to a topology with not enough executors and tasks to utilize all of them, we'd waste the precious resources by keeping them blocked and idle.

On the other hand, if we have a high number of workers and a high number of executors and tasks, the chances are that performance may degrade due to network latency.

Having stated these facts, I want to emphasize the fact that the performance tuning should be done cautiously and judiciously to arrive at what number works for the use case we are trying to implement.

The following screenshot captures the details about the supervisors, in terms of the statistics, with the corresponding information:

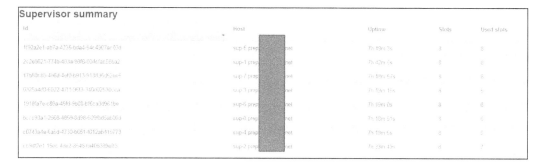

- Column one has the **Id** field for the supervisors, and column two has the names of the **hosts** field that have supervisor processes running.

- Column three captures the amount of time the supervisor has been running for.

- Columns five and six capture the number of slots available on the supervisor and the number of slots used respectively. These two numbers provide a very important metric in terms of how many slots are available and how many are used. They help us judge and understand what capacity the supervisors are operating at and how much bandwidth they have to handle the scenarios of failures; for instance, all my supervisors are operating at 100 percent capacity, so in that case, my cluster can't handle any failures.

The following screenshot is captured from the Storm UI depicting supervisors and their attributes:

supervisor.slots.ports	6700,6701,6702,6703,6704,6705,6706,6707,6706,6707
supervisor.worker.start.timeout.secs	120
supervisor.worker.timeout.secs	30
task.heartbeat.frequency.secs	3

The preceding section gives us details about the supervisor slots, timeouts, and so on. These values are specified on `storm.yaml`, but can be verified from the UI. For example, `http:// ip of nimbus:8080` in my case is `http://10.4.2.122:8080`, and my UI process executes on the Nimbus machine that has this IP: 10.4.2.122, as shown in the following screenshot:

Activate | Deactivate | Rebalance | Kill

Topology stats

Window	Emitted	Transferred	Complete latency (ms)	Acked	Failed
10m 0s	0	0	0.000	0	0
3h 0m 0s	0	0	0.000	0	0
1d 0h 0m 0s	12	15	22.000	3	0
All time	180	225	59.911	45	0

Spouts (All time)

Id	Executors	Tasks	Emitted	Transferred	Complete latency (ms)	Acked	Failed	Last error
AMQP_Spout	2	2	45	45	59.911	45	0	

Bolts (All time)

Id	Executors	Tasks	Emitted	Transferred	Capacity (last 10m)	Execute latency (ms)	Executed	Process latency (ms)	Acked	Failed	Last error
bolt	2	2	0	0	0.000	0.000	0	0.000	0	0	
ra_bolt	2	2	0	0	0.000	0.000	0	0.000	0	0	
or_bolt	2	2	0	0	0.000	4.578	45	4.489	45	0	
y_bolt	1	1	0	0	0.000	4.844	45	4.778	45	0	
s_device_bolt	2	2	0	0	0.000	0.000	0	0.000	0	0	

Now in the section depicted in the following screenshot one can get into by drilling deeper into the topology details. This can be achieved on the Storm UI by clicking on any of the topology names. This section holds the details about the components of the topology including the level of bolts, spouts, and details about them, as shown in the following screenshot:

Bolts (All time)

Id	Executors	Tasks	Emitted	Transferred	Capacity (last 10m)	Execute latency (ms)	Executed	Process latency (ms)	Acked	Failed	Last error
bolt	2	2	0	0	0.000	0.000	0	0.000	0	0	
bolt	2	2	0	0	0.000	1.341	34173	1.303	34173	0	
loud_bolt	1	1	0	0	0.000	0.000	0	0.000	0	0	
bolt	1	1	0	0	0.000	0.000	0	0.000	0	0	
	1	1	0	0	0.000	8.767	32674	8.720	32674	0	
cassandra_bolt	2	4	0	0	0.000	24.750	4	24.750	4	0	
bolt	2	2	23236	34864	0.000	65.614	17310	65.573	17310	0	
bolt	2	2	32481	32935	0.000	3.683	32076	3.637	32076	0	
	4	4	396068	396068	0.000	0.382	5333814	0.346	5333814	0	
cass_device_bolt	1	1	0	0	0.000	9.750	4	9.500	4	0	
faulting_bolt	3	6	2	2	0.000	0.375	12128	0.342	12128	0	

The preceding screenshot has details ranging from the number of executors or tasks allocated to each component, to the number of tuples emitted by the bolts or spouts and the number of tuples transferred to the next component in the **Directed Acyclic Graph (DAG)**.

Other notable details one should observe on the topology detail page are as follows:

- **Capacity** of bolts in the last 10 minutes: This should be well below 1.
- **Execute latency** is time in milliseconds: This determines how long it would take to execute a tuple through this component. If this value is too high, then we would probably want to break the execution into two or more bolts to utilize parallelism and have better efficiency.
- **Executed**: This stores the number of tuples executed successfully by this component.
- **Process latency**: This value displays the average total time taken to execute a tuple by the component. This value should be analyzed with the execute latency. These are practical cases that may happen:
  - **Execute latency** and **Process latency** are both low (that's the best possible case)
  - **Execute latency** is low but process latency is very high (that means actual execution time is lower in comparison to the total execution time and increasing parallelism might help achieve efficiency)
  - Both **Execute latency** and **Process latency** are high (again, increasing parallelism might help)

Storm logs

The next place to debug if things don't go as expected is the Storm log. First of all, one needs to know the location for Storm logs, which also update the path on `cluster.xml` at `storm-0.9.2-incubating.zip\apache-storm-0.9.2-incubating\logback\cluster.xml`:

```
<appender class="ch.qos.logback.core.rolling.RollingFileAppender"
  name="A1">
  <!--update this as below
  <file>${storm.home}/logs/${logfile.name}</file> -->
  <file>/mnt/app_logs/storm/storm_logs/${logfile.name}</file>
  <rollingPolicy
  class="ch.qos.logback.core.rolling.FixedWindowRollingPolicy">
    <fileNamePattern>${storm.home}/logs/${logfile.name}.%i
    </fileNamePattern>
    <minIndex>1</minIndex>
    <maxIndex>9</maxIndex>
</rollingPolicy>
```

```
<triggeringPolicy
  class="ch.qos.logback.core.rolling.SizeBasedTriggeringPolicy">
    <maxFileSize>100MB</maxFileSize>
</triggeringPolicy>
  <encoder>
    <pattern>%d{yyyy-MM-dd HH:mm:ss} %c{1} [%p] %m%n</pattern>
  </encoder>
</appender>
```

Now the line in bold gets you the path/location where the Storm logs will be created. Let's take a closer look to find out what kinds of logs are created by different Storm daemons.

The Nimbus node logs can be obtained by using the following commands on shell:

Cd /mnt/my_logs/strom/storm_logs
ls-lart

The listing of the Nimbus log directory is shown in the following screenshot:

```
total 1876
drwxr-xr-x 4 root root    4096 Nov 15 13:41 ..
-rw-r--r-- 1 root root       0 Dec 12 12:07 access.log
-rw-r--r-- 1 root root       0 Dec 12 12:07 metrics.log
drwxr-xr-x 2 root root    4096 Dec 12 12:07 .
-rw-r--r-- 1 root root 1667689 Dec 21 15:28 nimbus.log
-rw-r--r-- 1 root root  229733 Dec 26 16:16 ui.log
```

Notice that we have nimbus.log, which has details about Nimbus' startup, error, and info logs; ui.log is created on the node where we start the Storm UI application.

The logs on the supervisor nodes can be obtained by using the following commands on shell:

Cd /mnt/my_logs/strom/storm_logs
ls-lart

The listing of the supervisor log directory is shown in the following screenshot:

```
total 3916296
drwxr-xr-x 2 root root      4096 Dec 27 10:19 ./
drwxr-xr-x 4 root root      4096 Dec 12 12:23 ../
-rw-r--r-- 1 root root         0 Dec 12 12:25 access.log
-rw-r--r-- 1 root root       438 Dec 12 18:26 logviewer.log
-rw-r--r-- 1 root root         0 Dec 12 12:25 metrics.log
-rw-r--r-- 1 root root    558845 Dec 18 06:44 supervisor.log
-rw-r--r-- 1 root root    125789 Dec 12 18:34 worker-6700.log
-rw-r--r-- 1 root root    192106 Dec 17 20:12 worker-6701.log
-rw-r--r-- 1 root root    461346 Dec 17 20:11 worker-6702.log
-rw-r--r-- 1 root root  58919239 Dec 17 20:11 worker-6703.log
-rw-r--r-- 1 root root  82827339 Dec 27 10:25 worker-6704.log
-rw-r--r-- 1 root root 104906158 Dec 27 10:16 worker-6704.log.1
-rw-r--r-- 1 root root 104883747 Dec 27 09:59 worker-6704.log.2
```

One can see supervisor logs and worker logs. The supervisor logs capture the details about the supervisor starting up, any errors, and so on. The worker logs are the ones where the developer's topology logs appear along with Storm logs for various bolts and spouts.

So if we want to troubleshoot the Storm daemon processes, we would look at `nimbus.log` and `supervisor.log`. If you're having issues, then you need to debug using the corresponding worker log. The scenario of nimbus and worker node failures has been covered in *Chapter 4, Storm in a Clustered Mode*.

Now let's imagine a scenario. I am a developer whose topology is not behaving as expected, and I doubt that one of the bolts is not functioning as expected. So we need to debug the worker logs and find the root cause. Now we need to find out which worker log to look at out of multiple supervisors and numerous worker logs; we'll get this information from the Storm UI. Perform the following steps:

1. Open **Storm UI** and click on the troublesome topology.
2. Click on the suspected bolt or spout of the topology. A screen analogous to what is shown in this screenshot should appear:

Here is the clue to debug what's happening in this bolt; I will look into `Supervisor5` and `Supervisor6`, of `worker-6705.log` on `supervisor5` and `supervisor6`.

Quiz time

Q.1. State whether the following statements are true or false:

1.   Storm nodes can't be added to the cluster with topologies being executed.

2.   A topology can't survive the Storm node failure.

3.   Storm logs are created on each node in the cluster.

4.   The location of the Storm log creation is configurable.

Q.2. Fill in the blanks:

1.   _____ is the heartbeat tracker of the cluster.

2.   _____ is the daemon that's mandatory for topology submission and rebalancing.

3.   The _____ file holds the worker configuration for the topology.

Q.3. Execute the following use cases to see the internals of Storm:

1.   Start nimbus and check `nimbus.log` to see what a successful startup should look like.

2.   Start the supervisor and check `Supervisor.log` to see what a successful startup should look like.

3.   Submit the topology, say a simple `WordCount` topology, and figure out the `worker.log` file creation.

4.   Update `log4j.properties` to change the logging level and verify its impact.

Summary

In this chapter, we have covered the maintenance concepts of Storm in terms of adding new nodes, rebalancing, and killing topologies. We have understood and tweaked internals such as `numtasks` and parallelism in combination with to `numworkers` and network latency. You learned to locate and decipher logs of Storm components. You also understood the metrics of the Storm UI and their implications on topology performance.

In the next chapter, we will discuss advanced concepts of Storm, including micro-batching and Trident APIs.

10
Advance Concepts in Storm

In this chapter, we will cover the following topics:

- Building a Trident topology
- Understanding the Trident API
- Examples and illustrations

In this chapter, we will learn about transactional topologies and the Trident API. We will also explore the aspects of micro-batching and its implementation in Storm topology.

Building a Trident topology

Trident gives a batching edge to the Storm computation. It lets developers use the abstracted layer for computations over the Storm framework, giving the advantage of stateful processing with high throughput for distributed queries.

Well the architecture of Trident is the same as Storm; it's built on top of Storm to abstract a layer that adds the functionality of micro-batching and execution of SQL-like functions on top of Storm.

For the sake of analogy, one can say that Trident is a lot like Pig for batch processing in terms of concept. It has support for joins, aggregates, grouping, filters, functions, and so on.

Trident has basic batch processing features such as consistent processing and execution of process logic over the tuples exactly once.

Now to understand Trident and its working; let's look at a simple example.

The example we have picked up would achieve the following:

- Word count over the stream of sentences (a standard Storm word count kind of topology)
- A query implementation to get the sum of counts for a set of listed words

Here is the code for dissection:

```
FixedBatchSpout myFixedspout = new FixedBatchSpout(new
    Fields("sentence"), 3,
new Values("the basic storm topology do a great job"),
new Values("they get tremendous speed and guaranteed processing"),
new Values("that too in a reliable manner "),
new Values("the new trident api over storm gets user more features
    "),
new Values("it gets micro batching over storm "));
myFixedspout.setCycle(true);
```

This preceding code snippet ensures that the spout myFixedspout cycles over the set of sentences added as values. This snippet ensures that we have an endless flow of data streams into the topology and enough points to perform all micro-batching functions that we intend to.

Now we have made sure about continuous input stream let's look at the following snippet:

```
//creating a new trident topology
TridentTopology myTridentTopology = new TridentTopology();
//Adding a spout and configuring the fields and query
TridentState myWordCounts = topology.newStream("myFixedspout",
    spout)
    .each(new Fields("sentence"), new Split(), new Fields("word"))
    .groupBy(new Fields("word"))
    .persistentAggregate(new MemoryMapState.Factory(), new Count(),
    new Fields("count"))
    .parallelismHint(6);
```

Now let's look at the code line by line to interpret how it works.

Here we start with creating a Trident topology object, which in turn gets the developer access to the Trident interfaces.

This topology, myTridentTopology, has access to a method called newStream that enables it to create a new stream to read the data from the source.

Here we use `myFixedSpout` from the preceding snippet that would cycle through a predefined set of sentences. In a production scenario or a real-life scenario, we will use a spout to read the streams off a queue (such as RabbitMQ, Kafka, and so on).

Now the micro-batching; who does it and how? Well the Trident framework stores the state for each source (it kind of remembers what input data it has consumed so far). This state saving is done in the Zookeeper cluster. The tagging *spout* in the preceding code is actually a znode, which is created in the Zookeeper cluster to save the state metadata information.

This metadata information is stored for small batches wherein the batch size is a variant based on the speed of incoming tuples; it could be few hundred to millions of tuples based on the event **transactions per second (tps)**.

Now my spout reads and emits the stream into the field labeled as `sentence`. In the next line, we will split the sentence into words; that's the very same functionality that we deployed in our earlier reference to the `wordCount` topology.

The following is the code context capturing the working of the `split` functionality:

```
public class Split extends BaseFunction {
  public void execute(TridentTuple tuple, TridentCollector
  collector) {
      String sentence = tuple.getString(0);
      for(String word: sentence.split(" ")) {
          collector.emit(new Values(word));
      }
  }
}
```

A very simple context splits the sentence on *white space* to emit each word as a tuple.

Now the topology beyond this point computes the count and stores the results in a persistent manner. The topology can be computed by using the following steps:

1. We group the stream by the *word* field.
2. We aggregate and persist each group using the count aggregator.

The persistent function should be written in a fashion to store the results of aggregation in a store that's actually persisting the state. The illustration in the preceding code keeps all the aggregates in memory, this snippet can be very conveniently rewritten to persist the values to IMDB in memory database systems such as memcached or Hazelcast, or stable storage such as Cassandra and so on.

Trident with Storm is so popular because it guarantees the processing of all tuples in a fail-safe manner in exactly one semantic. In situations where retry is necessary because of failures, it does that exactly once and once only, so as a developer I don't end up updating the table storage multiple times on occurrence of a failure.

Trident works on micro-batching by creating very small batches on incoming streams, as shown in the following figure:

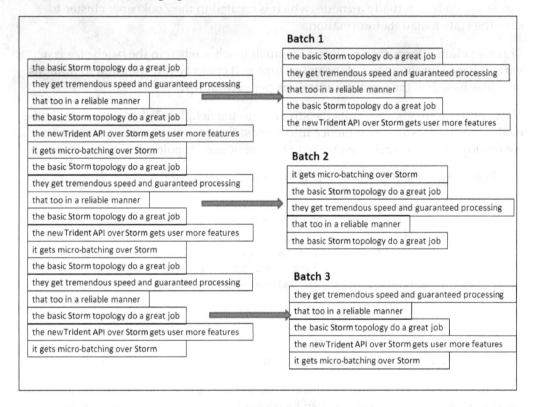

In the preceding figure, we have given a clear demonstration for micro-batching, how small batches are created over the streaming data by the Trident framework in Storm. Please remember, the preceding figure is just an illustration of micro-batching; the actual number of tuples in a batch is dependent on the tps of the incoming data on the source and is decided by the framework.

Now having achieved the micro-batching part of the problem, let's move on to the next part of the problem that is executing distributed queries on these micro batches. Trident Storm guarantees these queries to be low latency and lightning fast. In processing and semantics, these queries are very much like **Remote Procedure Call (RPC)**, but the distinction of Storm is that it gets you a high degree of parallelism, thus making them high performance and lightning fast in their execution.

Let's have a look at integration of such DRPC-based queries with our Trident components.

The following is a code snippet for DRPC followed by an explanation:

```
myTridentTopology.newDRPCStream("words")
    .each(new Fields("args"), new Split(), new Fields("word"))
    .groupBy(new Fields("word"))
    .stateQuery(wordCounts, new Fields("word"), new MapGet(), new
    Fields("count"))
    .each(new Fields("count"), new FilterNull())
    .aggregate(new Fields("count"), new Sum(), new Fields("sum"));
```

In the preceding code snippet, we created a DRPC stream using `myTridentTopology` and over and above it, we have a function named `word`.

Each of the DRPC query requests are treated as its own mini batch processing job, the two arguments that do this mini job is a single tuple representing the request. For instance, in our case, the argument is a list of words separated using a space.

Here are the steps that are being executed in the previous code snippet:

- We split the argument stream into its constituent words; for example, my argument, `storm trident topology`, is split into individual words such as `storm`, `trident`, and `topology`

- Then the incoming stream is grouped by `word`

- Next, the state-query-operator is used to query the Trident-state-object that was generated by the first part of the topology:

    ◦ State query takes in the word counts computed by an earlier section of the topology.

    ◦ It then executes the function as specified as part of the DRPC request to query the data.

    ◦ In this case, my topology is executing the `MapGet` function on the query to get the count of each word; the DRPC stream, in our case, is grouped in exactly the same manner as the `TridentState` in the preceding section of the topology. This arrangement guarantees that all my word count queries for each word are directed to the same Trident state partition of the `TridentState` object that would manage the updates for the word.

- `FilterNull` ensures that the words that don't have a count are filtered out

- The sum aggregator then sums all the counts to get the results, which are automatically returned back to the awaiting client

Having understood the execution as per the developer-written code, let's take a look at what's boilerplate to Trident and what happens automatically behind the scenes when this framework executes.

- We have two operations in our Trident word count topology that read from or write to state—`persistentAggregate` and `stateQuery`. Trident employs the capability to batch these operations automatically to that state. So for instance, the current processing requires 10 reads and writes to the database; Trident would automatically batch them together as one read and one write. This gets you performance and ease of computation where the optimization is handled by the framework.

- Trident aggregators are other highly efficient and optimized components of the framework. They don't work by the rule to transfer all the tuples to one machine and then aggregate, instead they optimize the computation by executing partial aggregations wherever possible and then transfer the results over the network, thus saving on network latency. The approach employed here is similar to combiners of the MapReduce world.

Understanding the Trident API

Trident API supports five broad categories of operations:

- Operations for manipulations of partitioning local data without network transfer

- Operations related to the repartitioning of the stream (involves the transfer of stream data over the network)

- Data aggregation over the stream (this operation do the network transfer as a part of operation)

- Grouping over a field in the stream

- Merge and join

Local partition manipulation operation

As the name suggests, these operations are locally operative over the batch on each node and no network traffic is involved for it. The following functions fall under this category.

Functions

- This operation takes single input value and emits zero or more tuples as the output

- The output of these function operations is appended to the end of the original tuple and emitted to the stream

- In cases where the function is such that no output tuple is emitted, the framework filters the input tuple too, while in other cases the input tuple is duplicated for each of the output tuples

Let's illustrate how this works with an example:

```
public class MyLocalFunction extends BaseFunction {
  public void execute(TridentTuple myTuple, TridentCollector
  myCollector) {
      for(int i=0; i < myTuple.getInteger(0); i++) {
          myCollector.emit(new Values(i));
      }
  }
}
```

Now the next assumption, the input stream in the variable called `myTridentStream` has the following fields `["a", "b", "c" ]` and the tuples on the stream are depicted as follows:

```
[10, 2, 30]
[40, 1, 60]
[30, 0, 80]
```

Now, let's execute the sample function created in the preceding code, as shown in the following code snippet:

```
mystream.each(new Fields("b"), new MyLocalFunction(), new
  Fields("d")))
```

The output expected here is as per the function it should return `["a", "b", "c", "d"]`, so for the preceding tuples in the stream I would get the following output:

```
//for input tuple [10, 2, 30] loop in the function executes twice
  //value of b=2
[10, 2, 30, 0]
[10, 2, 30, 1]
//for input tuple [4, 1, 6] loop in the function executes once
  value //of b =1
[4, 1, 6, 0]
//for input tuple [3, 0, 8]
//no output because the value of field b is zero and the for loop
  //would exit in first iteration itself value of b=0
```

Filters

Filters are no misnomers; their execution is exactly the same as their name suggests: they help us decide whether or not we have to keep a tuple or not—they do exactly what filters do, that is, remove what is not required as per a given criteria.

Let's have a look at the following snippet to see a working illustration of filter functions:

```
public class MyLocalFilterFunction extends BaseFunction {
    public boolean isKeep(TridentTuple tuple) {
        return tuple.getInteger(0) == 1 && tuple.getInteger(1) == 2;
    }
}
```

Let's look at the sample tuples on the input stream with the fields as ["a" , "b" , "c"]:

```
[1,2,3]
[2,1,1]
[2,3,4]
```

We execute or call the function as follows:

```
mystream.each(new Fields("b", "a"), new MyLocalFilterFunction())
```

The output would be as follows:

```
//for tuple 1 [1,2,3]
// no output because valueof("field b") ==1 && valueof("field a")
  ==2 //is not satisfied
//for tuple 1 [2,1,1]
// no output because valueof("field b") ==1 && valueof("field a")
  ==2 [2,1,1]
//for tuple 1 [2,3,4]
// no output because valueof("field b") ==1 && valueof("field a")
  ==2 //is not satisfied
```

partitionAggregate

The `partitionAggregate` function on each of the partitions over a set of tuples clubbed together as a batch. There is a behavioral difference between this function; compared to local functions that we have executed so far, this one emits a single output tuple for the stream on input tuples.

The following are other functions that can be used for various aggregates that can be executed over this framework.

Sum aggregate

Here is how the call is made to the sum aggregator function:

```
mystream.partitionAggregate(new Fields("b"), new Sum(), new
Fields("sum"))
```

Let's assume the input stream has the `["a", "b"]` fields, and the following are the tuples:

```
Partition 0:
["a", 1]
["b", 2]
Partition 1:
["a", 3]
["c", 8]
Partition 2:
["e", 1]
["d", 9]
["d", 10]
```

The output will be as follows:

```
Partition 0:
[3]
Partition 1:
[11]
Partition 2:
[20]
```

CombinerAggregator

The implementation of this interface provided by the Trident API returns a single tuple with a single field as an output; internally, it executes an init function on each input tuple and then after that it combines the values until only one value is left, which is returned as an output. If the combiner functions encounter a partition that doesn't have any value, "0" is emitted.

Here is the interface definition and its contracts:

```
public interface CombinerAggregator<T> extends Serializable {
    T init(TridentTuple tuple);
    T combine(T val1, T val2);
    T zero();
}
```

The following is the implementation for the count functionality:

```
public class myCount implements CombinerAggregator<Long> {
    public Long init(TridentTuple mytuple) {
        return 1L;
    }
public Long combine(Long val1, Long val2) {
        return val1 + val2;
    }

    public Long zero() {
        return 0L;
    }
}
```

The biggest advantage these CombinerAggregators functions have over the partitionAggregate function is that it's a more efficient and optimized approach as it proceeds by performing partial aggregations before the transfer of results over the network.

ReducerAggregator

As the name suggests, this function produces an init value and then iterates over every tuple in the input stream to produce an output comprising of a single field and a single tuple.

The following is the interface contract for the ReducerAggregate interface:

```
public interface ReducerAggregator<T> extends Serializable {
    T init();
    T reduce(T curr, TridentTuple tuple);
}
```

Here is the implementation of this interface for count functionality:

```
public class myReducerCount implements ReducerAggregator<Long> {
    public Long init() {
        return 0L;
    }

    public Long reduce(Long curr, TridentTuple tuple) {
        return curr + 1;
    }
}
```

Aggregator

An `Aggregator` function is the most commonly used and versatile aggregator function. It has the ability to emit one or more tuples, and each can have any number of fields. They have the following interface signature:

```
public interface Aggregator<T> extends Operation {
    T init(Object batchId, TridentCollector collector);
    void aggregate(T state, TridentTuple tuple, TridentCollector
    collector);
    void complete(T state, TridentCollector collector);
}
```

The execution pattern is as follows:

- The `init` method is a predecessor to processing of every batch. It's called before the processing of each batch. On completion, it returns an object holding the state representation of the batch, and this is passed on to the subsequent aggregate and complete methods.

- Unlike the `init` method, the `aggregate` method is called once for every tuple in the batch partition. This method can store the state, and can emit the results depending upon functionality requirements.

- The complete method is like a postprocessor; it's executed at the end, when the batch partition has been completely processed by the aggregate.

The following is the implementation of the count as an aggregator function:

```
public class CountAggregate extends BaseAggregator<CountState> {
    static class CountState {
        long count = 0;
    }
    public CountState init(Object batchId, TridentCollector
    collector) {
        return new CountState();
    }
    public void aggregate(CountState state, TridentTuple tuple,
    TridentCollector collector) {
        state.count+=1;
    }
    public void complete(CountState state, TridentCollector
    collector) {
        collector.emit(new Values(state.count));
    }
}
```

Numerous times we run into implementations requiring multiple aggregators to be executing simultaneously. In such cases, the concept of chaining comes in handy. Thanks to this functionality in the Trident API, we can build an execution chain of aggregators to be executed over batches of incoming stream tuples. Here is an example of these kinds of chains:

```
myInputstream.chainedAgg()
        .partitionAggregate(new Count(), new Fields("count"))
        .partitionAggregate(new Fields("b"), new Sum(), new
        Fields("sum"))
        .chainEnd()
```

The execution of this chain would run the specified sum and count aggregator functions on each partition. The output would be a single tuple, with two fields holding the values of sum and count.

Operations related to stream repartitioning

As the name suggests, these stream repartitioning operations are related to the execution of functions to change the tuple partitions across the tasks. These operations involve network traffic and the results redistribute the stream, and can result in changes to an overall partitioning strategy thus impacting a number of partitions.

Here are the repartitioning functions provided by the Trident API:

- Shuffle: This executes a rebalance kind of functionality and it employs a random round robin algorithm for an even redistribution of tuples across the partitions.

- Broadcast: This does what the name suggests; it broadcasts and transmits each tuple to every target partition.

- partitionBy: This function works on hashing and mod on a set of specified fields so that the same fields are always moved to the same partitions. As an analogy, one can assume that the functioning of this is similar to the fields grouping that we learned about initially in Storm groupings.

- global: This is identical to the global grouping of streams in a Storm, and in this case, the same partition is chosen for all the batches.

- batchGlobal: All tuples in a batch are sent to the same partition (so they kind of stick together), but different batches can be delivered to different partitions.

Data aggregations over the streams

Storm's Trident framework provides two kinds of operations for performing aggregations:

- `aggregate`: We have covered this in an earlier section, and it works in isolated partitions without involving network traffic

- `persistentAggregate`: This performs aggregate across partitions, but the difference is that it stores the results in a source of state

Grouping over a field in a stream

Grouping operations work in analogy to group by the operations in a relational model with the only differential being that the ones in the Storm framework execute over a stream of tuples from the input source.

Let's understand this more closely with the help of the following figure:

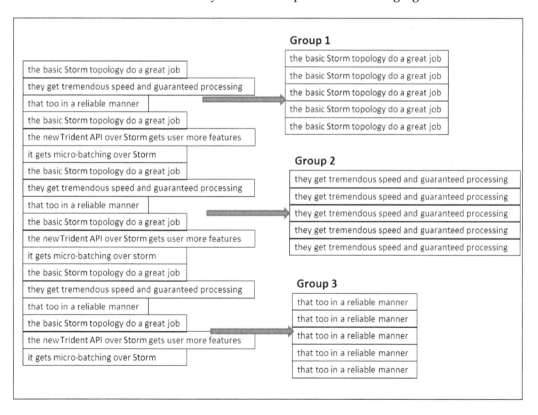

These operations in the Storm Trident run over a stream of tuples of several different partitions.

Merge and join

The merges and joins APIs provide interfaces for merging and joining various streams together. This is possible using a variety of ways provided as follows:

- Merge: As the name suggests, merge merges two or more streams together and emits the merged stream as the output field of the first stream:

  myTridentTopology.merge(stream1,stream2,stream3);

- Join: This operation works as the traditional SQL join function, but with the difference that it applies to small batches instead of entire infinite streams coming out of the spout

For example, consider a join function where Stream 1 has fields such as ["key", "val1", "val2"] and Stream 2 has ["x", "val1"], and from these functions we execute the following code:

```
myTridentTopology.join(stream1, new Fields("key"), stream2, new
    Fields("x"), new Fields("key", "a", "b", "c"));
```

As a result, Stream 1 and Stream 2 would be joined using key and x, wherein key would join the field for Stream 1 and x would join the field for Stream 2.

The output tuples emitted from the join would have the following:

- The list of all the join fields; in our case, it would be key from Stream 1 and x from Stream 2.
- A list of all the fields that are not join fields from all the streams involved in the join operation in the same order as they are passed to the join operation. In our case, it's a and b respectively for val1 and val2 of Stream 1, and c for val1 from Stream 2 (note that this step also removes the ambiguity of field names if any ambiguity is present within the stream, in our case val1 field was ambiguous between both the streams).

When operations like join happen on streams that are being fed in the topology from different spouts, the framework ensures that the spouts are synchronized with respect to batch emission, so that every join computation can include tuples from a batch of each spout.

Examples and illustrations

One of the other out-of-the-box and popular implementations of Trident is reach topology, which is a pure DRPC topology that finds the reach of a URL on demand. Let's first understand some of the jargon before we delve deeper.

Reach is basically a sum total of the count of Twitter users exposed to a URL.

Reach computation is a multistep process that can be attained by the following examples:

- Get all the users who have ever tweeted a URL
- Fetch the follower tree of each of these users
- Assemble the huge follower sets fetched previously
- Count the set

Well, looking at the skeletal algorithm entailed previously, you can make out that it is beyond the capability of a single machine and we'd need a distributed compute engine to achieve it. It's an ideal candidate of the Storm Trident framework, as you have the capability to execute highly parallel computations at each step across the cluster.

- Our Trident reach topology would be sucking data from two large data banks
- Bank A is the URL to the originator bank, wherein all the URLs would be stored along with the name of the user who had tweeted them
- Bank B is the user follower bank; this data bank will have a user to follow the mapping for all Twitter users

The topology would be defined as follows:

```
TridentState urlToTweeterState =
  topology.newStaticState(getUrlToTweetersState());
TridentState tweetersToFollowerState =
  topology.newStaticState(getTweeterToFollowersState());

topology.newDRPCStream("reach")
      .stateQuery(urlToTweeterState, new Fields("args"), new
      MapGet(), new Fields("tweeters"))
      .each(new Fields("tweeters"), new ExpandList(), new
      Fields("tweeter"))
      .shuffle()
      .stateQuery(tweetersToFollowerState, new Fields("tweeter"),
      new MapGet(), new Fields("followers"))
      .parallelismHint(200)
```

```
        .each(new Fields("followers"), new ExpandList(), new
        Fields("follower"))
        .groupBy(new Fields("follower"))
        .aggregate(new One(), new Fields("one"))
        .parallelismHint(20)
        .aggregate(new Count(), new Fields("reach"));
```

In the preceding topology, we perform the following steps:

1. Create a `TridentState` object for both data banks (URL to the originator Bank A and users to follow Bank B).

2. The `newStaticState` method is used for the instantiation of state objects for data banks; we have the capability to run the DRPC queries over the source states created earlier.

3. In execution, when the reach of a URL is to be computed, we perform a query using the Trident state for data bank A to fetch the list of all the users who have ever tweeted with this URL.

4. The `ExpandList` function creates and emits one tuple for each of the tweeters of the URL in query.

5. Next, we fetch the follower of each tweeter fetched previously. This step needs the highest degree of parallelism, thus we use shuffle grouping here for even load distribution across all instances of the bolt. In our reach topology, this is the most intense compute step.

6. Once we have the list of followers of the tweeter of the URL, we execute an operation analog to filter unique followers only.

7. We arrive at unique followers by grouping them together and then using the `one` aggregator. The latter simply emits 1 for each group and in the next step all these are counted together to arrive at the reach.

8. Then we count the followers (unique) thus arriving at the reach of the URL.

Quiz time

Q.1. State whether the following statements are true or false:

1. DRPC is a stateless, Storm processing mechanism.
2. If a tuple fails to execute in a Trident topology, the entire batch is replayed.
3. Trident lets the user implement windowing functions over streaming data.
4. Aggregators are more efficient then partitioned Aggregators.

Q.2. Fill in the blanks:

1. _____ is the distributed version of RPC.

2. _____ is the basic micro-batching framework over Storm.

3. The _____functions are used to remove tuples based on certain criteria or conditions from the stream batches.

Q.3. Create a Trident topology to find the tweeters who have the maximum number of tweets in the last 5 minutes.

Summary

In this chapter, we have pretty much covered everything about Storm and its advanced concepts with giving you the change to get hands-on with the Trident and DRPC topologies. You learned about Trident and its need and application, the DRPC topologies, and the various functions available in the Trident API.

In the next chapter, we will explore other technology components that go hand in hand with Storm and are necessary for building end-to-end solutions with Storm. We will touch upon areas of distributed caches and **Complex Event Processing (CEP)** with memcache and Esper in conjunction with Storm.

11
Distributed Cache and CEP with Storm

In this chapter, we will learn about the need for distributed caching in conjunction with Storm and the integration of widely used options with Storm. We will also touch upon the **Complex Event Processing (CEP)** engines in collaboration with Storm.

In this chapter, we will cover the following topics:

- The need for distributed caches in the Storm framework
- Introduction to memcache
- Building a topology with caches
- Introduction to CEP and Esper

At the end of this chapter, you should be able to apply CEP and cache in conjunction with Storm to solve real-time use cases.

The need for distributed caching in Storm

Now that we have explored Storm enough to understand all its strengths, let's touch on one of its biggest weaknesses: the lack of a shared cache, a common store in memory that all tasks running across the workers on various nodes in the Storm cluster can access and write to.

The following figure illustrates a three node Storm cluster where we have two workers running on each of the supervisor nodes:

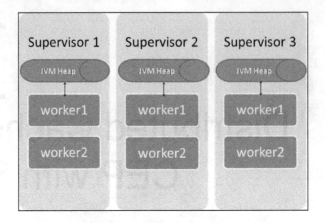

As depicted in the preceding figure, each worker has its own JVM where the data can be stored and cached. However, what we are missing here is a layer of cache that shares components within the workers on a supervisor as well as across the supervisors. The following figure depicts the need for what we are referring to:

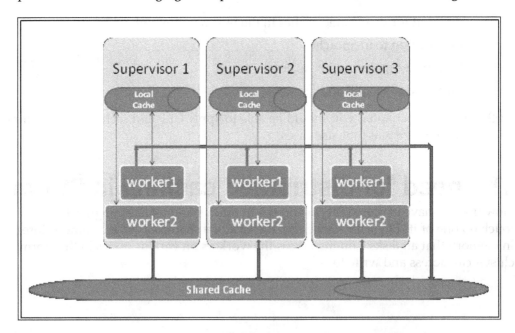

The preceding figure depicts the need for a shared caching layer where common data can be placed, which is referable from all nodes. These are very valid use cases because in production, we encounter scenarios such as the following:

- We have a lot of read-only reference dimensional data, which we would want in one place instead of having it replicated and updated at each supervisor level
- Sometimes, we have transactional data in certain use cases, which are to be read and updated by all the workers; for example, when counting certain events, the count has to be kept in a common location

This is where the layer of common shared cache that is accessible across all supervisor nodes comes in.

Introduction to memcached

Memcached is a very simple in-memory key value store; we can assume it to be an in-memory store for a hash map. This can be used in conjunction with Storm supervisors to serve as a common memory storage, which can be accessed for read/write operations by all the Storm workers on various nodes in the Storm cluster.

Memcached has the following components:

- The memcached server
- The memcache client
- The hashing algorithm (client-based implementation)
- The server algorithm for data retention

Memcached uses **Least Recently Used** (LRU) to discard the elements from the cache. This means that the items that have not been referred since the longest time are the first ones to be removed from the cache. These items are said to be expired from the cache, and if they are referred after expiry, they are reloaded from a stable storage.

The following is the flow of how entries are loaded and retrieved from or through a cache:

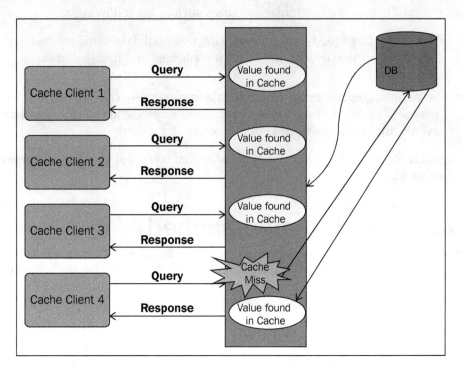

The preceding figure depicts the scenarios of cache hit and cache miss, where certain items expire as per the LRU algorithm. The scenarios in the preceding figure are as follows:

- When the cache app location starts, it's loaded with the data from the stable storage, in our case, from the database
- There are two scenarios that can happen in a situation where we request the data from the cache:
    - **Cache hit**: This is where the data we request exists on the cache server and in this case, the request is served from the cache
    - **Cache miss**: This is where the data requested doesn't exist in the cache server, and in this case, the data is fetched from the database into the cache and then the request is serviced from the cache

Now we understand how the cache functions and what the need for it in the context of solutions for Storm is.

Setting up memcache

The following are the steps that need to be executed and will be required for the installation of memcache:

```
wget http://memcached.org/latest
tar -zxvfmemcached-1.x.x.tar.gz
cdmemcached-1.x.x
./configure && make && make test &&sudo make install
```

The following is the code snippet to connect to the memcache client and functions. It retrieves the data from the cache:

```java
public class MemCacheClient {
  private static MemcachedClient client = null;
  private static final Logger logger =
  LogUtils.getLogger(MemCacheClient.class);

  /**
  * Constructor that accepts the cache properties as parameter
  and initialises the client object accordingly.
   * @param properties
   * @throws Exception
   */

  publicMemCacheClient(Properties properties) throws Exception {
    super();
    try {
      if (null == client) {
        client = new MemcachedClient(new InetSocketAddress(
          102.23.34.22,
          5454)));
      }
    } catch (IOException e) {
      if (null != client)
        shutdown();
      throw new Exception("Error while initiating MemCacheClient",
      e);
    }
  }

  /**
   * Shutdown the client and nullify it
   */
```

```java
public void shutdown() {
    logger.info("Shutting down memcache client ");
    client.shutdown();
    client = null;
}

/**
 * This method sets a value in cache with a specific key and
 timeout
 * @param key the unique key to identify the value
 * @paramtimeOut the time interval in ms after which the value
 would be refreshed
 * @paramval
 * @return
 */

public Future < Boolean > addToMemCache(String key, inttimeOut,
Object val) {
    if (null != client) {
        Future < Boolean > future = client.set(key, timeOut, val);
        return future;
    } else {
        return null;
    }
}

/**
 * retrives and returns the value object against the key passed
 in as parameter
 * @param key
 * @return
 */

public Object getMemcachedValue(String key) {
    if (null != client) {
        try {
            returnclient.get(key);
        } catch (OperationTimeoutException e) {
            logger.error(
                "Error while fetching value from memcache server for key "
                + key, e);
            return null;
        }
    } else
```

```
        return null;
    }
}
```

Once you encode the preceding snippet, you will have built the mechanism to create the cache client, load data into the cache, and retrieve values from it. So any Storm bolt that needs access to the cache can use the common layer created by memcache through interactions with the client.

Building a topology with a cache

Once we have the basic cache framework in place, it's very easy to plug it into the bolts and reference data from the cache or update it in the cache. Here is the snippet for the cache:

```
public class MyCacheReaderBolt extends BaseBasicBolt {
    MyCacheReadercacheReader;
    @Override
    public void prepare(Map stormConf, TopologyContext context) {
        super.prepare(stormConf, context);
        try {
            cacheReader = new MyCacheReader();
        } catch (Exception e) {
            logger.error("Error while initializing Cache", e);
        }
    }

    /**
        * Called whenever a new tuple is received by this bolt.
        Responsible for
        * emitting cache enriched event onto output stream
    */

    public void execute(Tuple tuple, BasicOutputCollector collector)
        {
        logger.info("execute method :: Start ");
        event = tuple.getString(0);
        populateEventFromCache(event);
        collector.emit(outputStream, new Values(event));
    } else {
        logger.warn("Event not parsed :: " + tuple.getString(0));
    }
```

```
    } catch (Exception e) {
      logger.error("Error in execute() ", e);
      }
    }
  logger.info("execute method :: End ");
  }

  private void populateEventFromCache(Event event) {
    HashMapfetchMap = (HashMap)
    cacheReader.get(searchObj.hashCode());
    if (null != fetchMap) {
      event.setAccountID(Integer.parseInt((String)
      fetchMap.get("account_id")));
      logger.debug("Populating event" + event + " using cache " +
      fetchMap);
    } else {
      logger.debug("No matching event found in cache.");
    }
    logger.info("Time to fetch from cache=" +
    (System.currentTimeMillis() - t1) + "msec");
    }
  }


  /**
   * Declares output streams and tuple fields emitted from this bolt
   */
   @Override
     public void declareOutputFields(OutputFieldsDeclarer declarer)
     {
     String stormStreamName = logStream.getName() + "_" +
     eventType;
     declarer.declareStream(stormStreamName, new
     Fields(stormStreamName));
    logger.debug("Topology : " + topology.getTopologyName() + ",
    Declared output stream : " + stormStreamName + ", Output field :
    " + stormStreamName);
  }
```

The preceding code snippet demonstrates a bolt, which reads an event from the
stream, gets some dimensional data from memcache, and emits the enriched bolt
to the streams to the following bolts in the DAG topology.

Introduction to the complex event processing engine

There are two terms that are generally used in conjunction; they are **Complex Event Processing (CEP)** and **Event Stream Processing (ESP)**.

Well, in theory, these are part of a technical paradigm that allow us to build applications with dramatic, real-time analytics over streaming data. They let us process incoming events at a very fast rate and execute SQL-like queries on top of the stream of events to generate real-time histograms. We can assume that CEP is an inversion of traditional databases. In the case of traditional DBMS and RDBMS, we have data stored, and then we run SQL queries over them to arrive at results, while in the case of CEPs, we have the queries predefined or stored and we run the data through them. We can envision this with an example; let's say I am running a department store and I would like to know the highest selling item in the last one hour. So if you look here, the query we are about to execute is pretty fixed in nature but the input data isn't constant—it changes at each sale transaction. Similarly, let's say I run a stock holding company and would like to know the top 10 performers over the last 2 minutes every 5 seconds.

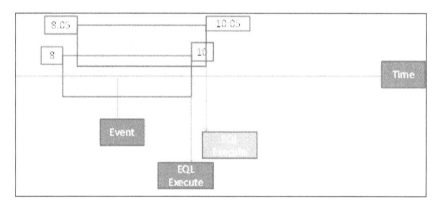

The preceding figure depicts the stock ticker use case where we have a sliding window of 2 minutes and the stock ticker is sliding every 5 seconds. We have many practical use cases for this nowadays, such as:

- Fraud detection patterns against **Point Of Sales (POS)** transactions
- Top N in any segment
- The application of deep learning patterns to stream data from any source

Now, having understood CEP and its need at a high level, let's touch upon its high-level components:

- The operand in every CEP is `Data` of `Event`; it's essentially an event-driven system

- **Event processing language**: This is the tool that facilitates the framing of queries to be executed on the data

- **Listeners**: These are the components that actually execute the query and perform the action on the arrival of the event into the system

Esper

Esper is one of the leading CEP engines that are available under open source—GPL and Enterprise License. The package can be downloaded from `http://www.espertech.com/download/`, and if you are attempting to execute a Maven-based Esper project, the dependency can be built as follows:

```
<dependency>
<groupId>com.espertech</groupId>
<artifactId>esper</artifactId>
<version> ... </version>
</dependency>
Ref :Espertech.com
```

The next obvious question could be why we want to use Esper-CEP in conjunction with Storm. Well, Esper has some unique capabilities that work well with Storm and let the EQL facility leverage the results drawn over Storm. The following are complementing features that lead to this choice:

- **Throughput**: Complementing the capability of Storm, Esper also has a very high throughput and can process from 1K to 100K messages per second.

- **Latency**: Esper has the ability to perform EQLs and actions based on results of Esper at a very low latency rate; in most cases, this is the order of milliseconds.

- **Computations**: These refer to the ability to perform functions such as pattern detection, complex queries based on aggregates, and correlation over time. These slice windows of streaming data.

Getting started with Esper

Before we start conjugating Esper and Storm, let's try a small do-it-yourself exercise on Esper alone to understand the structural components of the Esper as well as its wiring.

Let's build a case where we are attempting to get the list of scores above 10,000 in Roulette.

We expect you to download the Esper bundle from EsperTech (http://www. espertech.com/community/) on to your POM before starting the coding. Or, you can use the Maven dependency mentioned in the preceding section.

The following is the code snippet of the Esper event—in our example, this is CasinoWinEvent, a value object where we store the name of the game, the prize amount, and the timestamp:

```
public static class CasinoWinEvent {
  String game;
  Double prizeAmount;
  Date timeStamp;

  publicCasinoWinEvent(String s, double p, long t) {
    game = s;
    prizeAmount = p;
    timeStamp = new Date(t);
  }
  public double getPrizeAmount() {
    return prizeAmount;
  }
  public String getGame() {
    return game;
  }
  public Date getTimeStamp() {
    return timeStamp;
  }

  @
  Override
  public String toString() {
    return "Price: " + price.toString() + " time: " +
    timeStamp.toString();
  }
}
```

Once we have the value object in place, the next step is to instantiate the Esper engine and listener and wire in all the pieces together:

```
public class myEsperMain {
  private static Random generator = new Random();
  public static void GenerateRandomCasinoWinEvent(EPRuntimecepRT)
  {
    doubleprizeAmount = (double) generator.nextInt(10);
    longtimeStamp = System.currentTimeMillis();
    String game = "Roulette";
    CasinoWinEventcasinoEvent = new CasinoWinEvent(game,
    prizeAmount, timeStamp);
    System.out.println("Sending Event:" + casinoEvent);
    cepRT.sendEvent(casinoEvent);
  }
  public static class CEPListener implements UpdateListener {
    public void update(EventBean[] newData, EventBean[] oldData) {
      System.out.println("Event received: " +
      newData[0].getUnderlying());
    }
  }
  public static void main(String[] args) {
    //The Configuration is meant only as an initialization-time
    object.
    Configuration cepConfig = new Configuration();
    cepConfig.addEventType("CasinoEvent",
    CasinoWinEvent.class.getName());
    EPServiceProvidercep =
    EPServiceProviderManager.getProvider("myCEPEngine",
    cepConfig);
    EPRuntimecepRT = cep.getEPRuntime();
    EPAdministratorcepAdm = cep.getEPAdministrator();
    EPStatementcepStatement = cepAdm.createEPL("select * from " +
    "CasinoEvent(symbol='Roulette').win:length(2) " + "having
    avg(prizeAmount) > 10000.0");
```

```
        cepStatement.addListener(new CEPListener());
        // We generate a few ticks...
        for (inti = 0; i < 5; i++) {
          GenerateRandomCasinoWinEvent(cepRT);
        }
    }
}
```

Here is the snippet of the output:

```
log4j:WARN No appenders could be found for logger (com.espertech.esper.epl.metr
c.MetricReportingPath).
log4j:WARN Please initialize the log4j system properly.
Sending Event: prizeAmount: 1000.0 time: Tue Jan 21 01:11:15 PST 2015
Sending Event: prizeAmount: 0.0 time: Tue Jan 21 01:11:15 PST 2015
Sending Event: prizeAmount: 1007.0 time: Tue Jan 21 01:11:15 PST 2015
Sending Event: prizeAmount: 124.0 time: Tue Jan 21 01:11:15 PST 2015
Sending Event: prizeAmount: 20009.0 time: Tue Jan 21 01:11:15 PST 2015
Event received: prizeAmount: 20009.0 time: Tue Jan 21 01:11:15 PST 2015
```

In the preceding snippet, CEPListener is the implementation of updateListener (which listens for the arrival of the event), newData has the stream of one or more new arriving events, and oldData has the previous state of the stream, that is, before the arrival of the current trigger to the listener.

In the main method, we can load the Esper configuration or, as shown in our preceding case, create a default configuration. Then, we create an Esper runtime engine instance and bind the EQL query to it.

If you look at the cepStatement.addListener(new CEPListener()) statement in the preceding code, you will see that we are also binding the listener to the statement, thus wiring all the pieces together.

Integrating Esper with Storm

The following figure depicts how we plan to use Esper in conjunction with one of the topologies we created earlier in *Chapter 6, Adding NoSQL Persistence to Storm*. The integration of Storm with Esper gives the developer the power to execute SQL-like queries on top of the stream of events being processed by Storm.

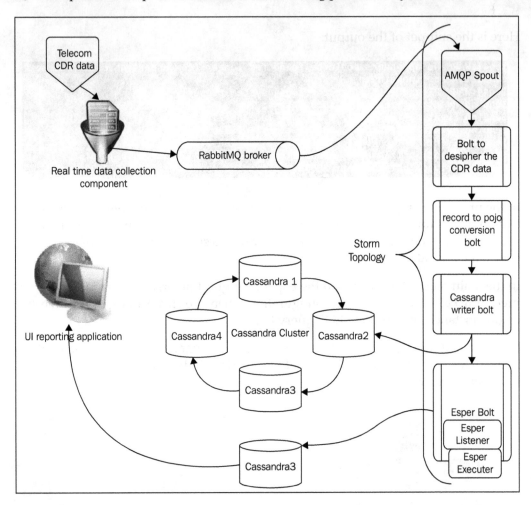

Here, we made some modifications to one of the earlier topologies that we created, and we added an Esper bolt to the same topology. This bolt reads the same stream that is being dumped into Cassandra and performs an EQL execution through Esperlistener. It executes to filter the set of records where the call duration is 0 seconds.

The following is a snippet from the `ZeroDuration` filter bolt that filters the `CALL_END` events that have a duration of 0 seconds to be emitted onto the stream feeding the Esper bolt:

```
/*
 * Bolt responsible for forwarding events which satisfy following
criteria:
 * <ul>
 * <li>event should belong to 'End'  type</li>
 * <li>duration should be zero</li>
 * </ul>
 */

public class ZeroSecondsCDRBolt extends BaseRichBolt {

    /**
     * Called when {@link ZeroSecondsCDRBolt} is initialized
     */
    @Override
    public void prepare(Map conf, TopologyContext context,
        OutputCollector collector) {
        logger.info("prepare method :: Start ");
        this.collector = collector;
        logger.info("prepare() conf {},Collector {}", conf.toString(),
        collector.toString());
        logger.info("prepare method :: End ");
    }

    /**
     * Called whenever a new tuple is received by this bolt. This
method
      * filters zero duration End records
      */

    @
    Override
    public void execute(Tuple tuple) {
        logger.info("execute method :: Start ");

        if (tuple != null && tuple.getString(0) != null) {
            eventCounter++;
            String event = tuple.getString(0);
            logger.info("execute :event recd :: {}", event);
            if (event != null && event.contains("CALL_END")) {
```

```
        emitCallEndRecords(tuple);
      }
      collector.ack(tuple);
    }
    logger.info("execute method :: End ");
}

  private void emitCallEndRecords(Tuple tuple) {
    String event = tuple.getString(0);

      try {
        //splitting the event based on semicolon
        String[] eventTokens = event.split(",");
        duration = Long.parseLong(eventTokens[4]);
        callId = Long.parseLong(eventTokens[0]);
        logger.debug(" Event (callId = {}) is a Zero duration
        Qualifier ", callId);
        collector.emit(....);

      } catch (Exception e) {
        logger.error("Corrupt Stopped record. Error occurred while
        parsing the event : {}", event);
      }
    }

  /**
  * Declares output fields in tuple emitted from this bolt
  */

  @Override
  public void declareOutputFields(OutputFieldsDeclarer declarer) {
    declarer.declareStream(CALL_END, new Fields());
  }

  @
  Override
  public Map < String, Object > getComponentConfiguration() {
    return null;
  }
}
```

The next step is to conjugate the Esper bolt into the topology. This can be easily downloaded as a bundle from https://github.com/tomdz/storm-esper, and it can be quickly bundled into the topology using the following code:

```
EsperBoltesperBolt = newEsperBolt.Builder()
    .inputs()
    .aliasComponent("ZeroSecondCallBolt")
    .withFields("a", "b")
    .ofType(Integer.class)
    .toEventType("CALL_END")
    .outputs()
    .outputs().onDefaultStream().emit("count")
    .statements()
    .add("select callID as CALL_ID,callType as CALL_TYPE, count(*)
    as OCCURRENCE_CNT from CDR.win:time_batch(5 minutes)  where
    (eventType = 'CALL_END') and (duration = 0) group by
    callID,eventType having count(*) > 0 order by
    OCCURRENCE_CNTdesc")
    .build();
```

Here is what the output would be like:

```
log4j:WARN No appenders could be found for logger (com.espertech.esper.epl.metric.MetricReportingPath).
log4j:WARN Please initialize the log4j system properly.
Tue Jan 21 01:11:15 PST 2015 Count of Zero byte records 7 in last 5 minutes
Tue Jan 21 01:11:16 PST 2015 Count of Zero byte records 9 in last 5 minutes
Tue Jan 21 01:11:17 PST 2015 Count of Zero byte records 15 in last 5 minutes
Tue Jan 21 01:11:18 PST 2015 Count of Zero byte records 12 in last 5 minutes
```

The Esper query in the preceding figure executes on a stream of incoming data; here is its breakdown and explanation:

```
selectcallID as CALL_ID,callType as CALL_TYPE, count(*) as
    OCCURRENCE_CNT
```

We are selecting the following fields from the incoming tuples, such as `Call_Id`, `Call_type`, and `count`:

```
fromCDR.win:time_batch(5 minutes)  where (eventType = 'CALL_END')
  and (duration = 0) group by callID,eventTypehaving count(*) > 0
order by OCCURRENCE_CNTdesc
```

The named window out of which we are operating is `CDR.WIN`. The batch size is 5 minutes, which means that with the arrival of every event or tuple, we are looking back into time for 5 minutes and executing the query over data that has arrived in the last 5 minutes. The results are grouped by the event type and are sorted in reverse order.

Quiz time

Q.1. State whether the following statements are true or false:

1. Cache is a read-only memory space.
2. Data once added in cache remains there forever.
3. CEP lets SQL-like queries be implemented over streaming data.
4. Esper is based on event-driven architecture.

Q.2. Fill in the blanks:

1. _____ is the algorithm for memcache.
2. When data is not present in the cache, it's called _____.
3. _____ is the component of Esper that triggers the **Endeca Query Language (EQL)** execution.
4. _____ is generally used for the time series windowing function data.

Q.3. Create an end-to-end topology using Esper to display the top 10 speeding devices on a said freeway using Storm and Esper in conjunction.

Summary

In this chapter, we covered the concept of cache in conjunction with Storm and the utility and application of the solutions developer with cache. We learned about memcache as a caching system.

In the later part of the chapter, we explored Esper as a complex event processing system and understood its integration with Storm topologies.

Quiz Answers

Chapter 1

Q.1.	Monitor the ping latency and raise an alert when it crosses a certain threshold to provide a real-time sensing of network.
	Monitor events from traffic sensors and plot a graph of choke points at peak hours of day.
	Sensing intrusions on borders.

Chapter 2

Q.1.	False
	False
	True
	False
Q.2.	Topology Builder
	Parallelism
	Nimbus

Chapter 3

Q.1.	True
	False
	True
	True
Q.2.	ack()
	declare()
	emit()

Chapter 4

Q.1.	True
	Flase
	False
	True
	True
Q.2.	Process latency
	Execute latency
	Zookeeper

Chapter 5

Q.1.	False
	False
	True
	True
Q.2.	Direct exchange
	Fan-out
	AMQP spout

Chapter 6

Q.1.	False
	False
	True
	False
Q.2.	AP
	Low write latency
	hector

Chapter 7

Q.1.	False
	False
	True
	True
Q.2.	Snitch
	ANY
	repair

Chapter 8

Q.1.	False
	False
	False
	False
Q.2.	Nodetool compact
	Ring
	Ring

Chapter 9

Q.1.	False
	False
	True
	True
Q.2.	Zookeeper
	Nimbus
	storm-config.xml

Chapter 10

Q.1.	False
	True
	True
	False
Q.2.	DRPC
	Trident
	filter

Chapter 11

Q.1.	False
	False
	True
	True
Q.2.	LRU
	cache-miss
	EPRuntime
	Timebatch window

Index

Z

zoo.cfg configuration file
  properties 23
Zookeeper
  about 9
  clean up script 47, 48
  configurations 46, 47
Zookeeper (v 3.3.5)
  setting up 22-25

Thank you for buying
Real-time Analytics with Storm and Cassandra

About Packt Publishing

Packt, pronounced 'packed', published its first book, *Mastering phpMyAdmin for Effective MySQL Management*, in April 2004, and subsequently continued to specialize in publishing highly focused books on specific technologies and solutions.

Our books and publications share the experiences of your fellow IT professionals in adapting and customizing today's systems, applications, and frameworks. Our solution-based books give you the knowledge and power to customize the software and technologies you're using to get the job done. Packt books are more specific and less general than the IT books you have seen in the past. Our unique business model allows us to bring you more focused information, giving you more of what you need to know, and less of what you don't.

Packt is a modern yet unique publishing company that focuses on producing quality, cutting-edge books for communities of developers, administrators, and newbies alike. For more information, please visit our website at www.packtpub.com.

About Packt Open Source

In 2010, Packt launched two new brands, Packt Open Source and Packt Enterprise, in order to continue its focus on specialization. This book is part of the Packt Open Source brand, home to books published on software built around open source licenses, and offering information to anybody from advanced developers to budding web designers. The Open Source brand also runs Packt's Open Source Royalty Scheme, by which Packt gives a royalty to each open source project about whose software a book is sold.

Writing for Packt

We welcome all inquiries from people who are interested in authoring. Book proposals should be sent to author@packtpub.com. If your book idea is still at an early stage and you would like to discuss it first before writing a formal book proposal, then please contact us; one of our commissioning editors will get in touch with you.

We're not just looking for published authors; if you have strong technical skills but no writing experience, our experienced editors can help you develop a writing career, or simply get some additional reward for your expertise.

[PACKT] open source *
PUBLISHING
community experience distilled

Storm Blueprints: Patterns for Distributed Real-time Computation

ISBN: 978-1-78216-829-4   Paperback: 336 pages

Use Storm design patterns to perform distributed, real-time big data processing, and analytics for real-world use cases

1. Process high-volume log files in real time while learning the fundamentals of Storm topologies and system deployment.

2. Deploy Storm on Hadoop (YARN) and understand how the systems complement each other for online advertising and trade processing.

3. Follow along as each chapter presents a new problem and the architectural pattern, design, and implementation of a solution.

Storm Real-time Processing Cookbook

ISBN: 978-1-78216-442-5   Paperback: 254 pages

Efficiently process unbounded streams of data in real time

1. Learn the key concepts of processing data in real time with Storm.

2. Concepts ranging from Log stream processing to mastering data management with Storm.

3. Written in a Cookbook style, with plenty of practical recipes with well-explained code examples and relevant screenshots and diagrams.

Please check **www.PacktPub.com** for information on our titles

Learning Storm

ISBN: 978-1-78398-132-8   Paperback: 252 pages

Create real-time stream processing applications with Apache Storm

1. Integrate Storm with other Big Data technologies like Hadoop, HBase, and Apache Kafka.

2. Explore log processing and machine learning using Storm.

3. Step-by-step and easy-to-understand guide to effortlessly create applications with Storm.

Mastering Apache Cassandra

ISBN: 978-1-78216-268-1   Paperback: 340 pages

Get comfortable with the fastest NoSQL database, its architecture, key programming patterns, infrastructure management, and more!

1. Complete coverage of all aspects of Cassandra.

2. Discusses prominent patterns, pros and cons, and use cases.

3. Contains briefs on integration with other software.

Please check **www.PacktPub.com** for information on our titles

www.ingramcontent.com/pod-product-compliance
Lightning Source LLC
Chambersburg PA
CBHW060555060326
40690CB00017B/3713